TALES FROM THE COFFEE HOUSE

Stories about Lloyd's

By the same author

FAR FROM HUMDRUM

WILLIAM CHARLES CROCKER

Tales from the Coffee House

Stories about Lloyd's

LONDON
ROBERT HALE & COMPANY

First published in Great Britain 1973

ISBN 0 7091 3944 6

Robert Hale & Company
63 Old Brompton Road
London, S.W.7

Printed in Great Britain by
Clarke, Doble & Brendon Ltd.
Plymouth

CONTENTS

Contents

ILLUSTRATIONS

(Between pages 64 and 65)

ACKNOWLEDGEMENTS

I offer sincere thanks to those who have buttressed my memory with relevant data and for research carried out by them on my behalf. I single out among these helpers Mr. Edward G. Chapman, founder and long time Editor of *Lloyd's Log*, the executive officers of Lloyd's Information Department, and Mr. Joseph G. Rosa of The Salvage Association, London.

W.C.C.

ONE

MY FIRST VISIT TO LLOYD'S, 1907

BEFORE, for the first time in my life, I set foot in Lloyd's (this was in 1907) I had, in my mind's eye, but a dim vision of what to expect there. I knew, of course, that Lloyd's was an ancient institution, older indeed than the Bank of England, and since its birth in Edward Lloyd's Coffee House, had grown up to be not only the centre of the marine insurance world but a newcomer, a mere baby market, for the covering of risks on dry land. I had also learned that the risks insured at Lloyd's were carried, not as many thought, by the Corporation, but were split up among its individual 'underwriting' members. This meant that if an underwriter liked a risk 'shown' to him by a broker he would take such a percentage of it as he might think wise and this solely for his own account. And up to that limit (known as a 'line') his entire fortune was pledged to the honourable fulfilment of his obligation.

These few facts, the sum of my very general knowledge, did little to reveal how this insurance giant called Lloyd's actually operated.

Since the British notoriously cling to their old customs with a tenacity which now and then raises a laugh abroad I thought that at Lloyd's, with its roots in the distant past, the day's work would jog along much as it had done ever since the reign of Queen Anne. The layout of the Room above the Royal Exchange I guessed would have altered little from the view of it engraved for Ackerman's *Microcosm of London* in the eighteenth century. I was not to be disappointed, but once through the door my eyes opened upon a scene rather different from that which I had conjured up. True the layout at least was still good eighteenth century as Ackerman's artist had seen it; underwriters sat in their Coffee House Boxes at the receipt of custom. But here was no club-like atmosphere with sedate members conversing in undertones. Far from it! At the barrier I asked the attendant 'waiter' to call Mr. A. L. Royle, deputy to Mr. A. J. Whitcombe (my first Lloyd's client, bless him!). This request went by speaking-tube to the legendary 'caller', Farrant, a majestic figure scarlet-robed, heavily bearded and towering above everyone in his elevated rostrum.

Only a naturally gifted stentorian singer could have made himself heard above the prevailing noise, a very unclub-like murmur arising from hundreds of uninhibited conversations and the tread of innumerable feet moving back and forth on the Room's hard linoleum. Shortly after singing a dozen other calls Farrant reached mine. It emerged in a flow of harmonious syllables as 'AR-THUR WHIT-COMBE (pause) ROY-ALL' and this rising high-pitched ending fetched Royle to collect me almost immediately.

We went through the Room together from end to end. At many of the Boxes were queues of brokers waiting their turn to submit an insurance to the seated underwriter. For the most part these men chatted among themselves gaily, even laughingly—could it be at some side-splitting aspect of the York-Antwerp Rules or over a particularly amusing 'total loss'?

On none of their faces nor on those of the underwriters themselves were to be read signs of agitation, strain or apprehension such as one might well think would be shown by men involved as they were for example in the towering risks which threaten those "that go down to the sea in ships and occupy their business in great waters".

While pondering this, to me, surprising stoicism I happened to notice an elderly gentleman who stood, slightly bent, in a narrow passage way separating a long range of Boxes. He looked stern, determined and clearly moved by strong emotion. Was he an underwriter just warned of a shattering loss? Did the typed sheet he carried convey the bad news? Was it irritation and frustration which drove him to crush the paper into a ball to be thrown angrily away? No! I was wrong again! Popping up from cover he aimed the unoffending ball at the head of an underwriter two Boxes away, scored a bull and dropped down out of sight convulsed with laughter. Here was a revelation! Lloyd's men were not only stoics; *they had fun*!

TWO

INTRODUCING FRANCIS ROBERT BUSSELL

MY next sixty years at Lloyd's taught me a lot about the Insurance World. I saw that the slings and arrows of outrageous fortune are meat and drink to it. For mortals menaced by fire and flood, storm and tempest, disease and death, by perils on land and sea, by the forger, the thief, by those unwittingly defamed or damaged in body or property and by many another shaft aimed at the pocket, surely the best shield for the potential but prudent victim is a policy of insurance? The underwriters, with a shrewd time-tested idea of the odds, charge premiums which in bulk, over the years, will form a Pool deep enough to meet all the losses and leave a fair margin for profit. But the underwriter is always at risk that for a while the odds may run seriously against him and bring losses too big to suit his book. So he insures himself against that sort of happening, faithful to the vital Insurance principle which demands that in the end all losses shall be so widely spread across the market that even those headlined in the press as 'Catastrophic Disasters' leave the individual underwriter calm, solvent and ready for more. But a residual thought still irked me. Any Pool no matter how deep must eventually go dry if by ill chance the claims on it should continuously exceed the inflow of premiums. I put this thought to Francis Bussell.

"Yes," said he with his usual gentle smile, "it sounds like real good logic. But you miss two not unimportant points. In the first place a steady rise in losses brings a steady rise in premiums. The long history of insurance is one of waves and hollows. And in the second place, believe it or not, an immense loss which gets horrifying publicity is something of a blessing in disguise. It alerts the uninsured and the underinsured to their own vulnerability. They rush to us for cover. The result is that new premiums pour into our Pool from all over the world and the heavier the publicity the higher the flood. Your pal Shakespeare wrote something on the swings and roundabouts didn't he?"

"He did indeed," said I, "his words were 'There is some soul of goodness in things evil'."

* * *

For thirty years F.R.B. was my closest friend, mentor and benefactor. He had been dead for twenty years when I tried to set out his character in words. I wrote of him:

> " . . . he was a man so fine and rare that one could not bring him to life in cold print. His most marked trait was a modesty deep beyond belief. Shy, retiring, affectionate, full of quiet fun, doing much good by stealth and sinless as a saint, he thought his great success at Lloyd's was due solely to luck. All that he owed to luck was that with an underwriter for father he was destined to follow suit. His flair and his pluck made up the rest. . . ."[1]

None of those who knew him best ever hinted that this was a picture seen through rose-coloured glasses and touched with eulogy. In retrospect I feel there should have been more stress upon the charm of his companionship and his invariably tolerant, amused and unmalicious approach to life in all its facets. It is my hope that the following pages may in some degree amend that error.

[1] In my autobiography *Far from Humdrum* (Hutchinson) 1967.

THREE

F.R.B. ON LLOYD'S AND HIS AIDES, 'DEV' AND DANCEY

F. R. B. HAD a deep if unspoken affection for Lloyd's and all Lloyd's stood for. He once asked me if there was any other top-ranking institution where a lad from a poor locality with a mere Board School education and no outside influence could enter at the lowest level and by his own *nous* and industry reach the top.

After admitting that he himself had had a bit of schooling and an underwriter father (disadvantages which he implied he had fortuitously overcome) he told me a story about one of his own staff to illustrate this point.

I am not striving for chronological order in these random reminiscences and can only tie this specific story to an early period in Francis' career when his work was building up at embarrassing speed. He thought by finding a likely lad, a sort of pupil, who would sit in the Box and learn to handle many of the simpler but necessary routine matters the load might be eased.

Hartley Cooper and Co., Francis' principals, who had him under contract to underwrite for their Non-Marine Syndicate, ran a steady messenger service back and forth between the Room and their City offices. Francis noticed that of two new youngsters being used in this capacity one of them, with an open face and a quiet manner, seemed to be just the 'pupil' type he had in mind and he phoned Hartley Cooper's secretary to that effect.

The lad, told of this chance to switch jobs, leapt at it

and sped across to Lloyd's to report for duty. But the secretary had blundered. *This was the wrong lad!*

Francis, ever gentle and compassionate, could not find it in his heart to correct the mistake. He decided instead to accept, for what he might be worth, this tall, tough young Londoner with the strong, smiling face and the forthright Cockney accent. There was never a happier blunder. George A. Deverell showed his worth at once. He had a striking gift for figures, a faultless memory, an impulsive drive to learn everything worth learning, a natural 'feel' for insurance and a pawky wit which put him in the good graces of all those with whom he rubbed shoulders. With such an appreciative chief as Francis at his back it was ordained that 'Dev' would one day, if to his stunned surprise, be made a member of the F.R.B. Syndicate and deputy to A. H. Dancey who was then in charge of the Box under Francis' remote control. And much later, when Dancey retired, 'Dev' stepped into his shoes, thus exemplifying Francis' contention, that at Lloyd's a boy with negligible education and no push from the Establishment could start at the bottom and climb to the top.

'Dev's' idiom had never been ungrammatical. Neither in speaking nor on paper was he ever less than crystal clear. But as a matter of pride, call it inverted snobbery, he clung as best he could to his natal Cockney accent, an accent which, alas!, gradually deteriorated through his daily exposure to the voices of so many men who, unlike him, had attended such indifferent seats of learning as Eton, Winchester and Magdalen.

* * *

A. H. Dancey was a child musician of genius. He played the piano when his legs were too short to let him reach the pedals. Wooden blocks bridged the gap. His beautiful voice gave him a free place in St. Paul's Cathedral Choir School and brought him frequently in contact with one of its strongest patrons, Sir Ernest Cooper, a founder of Hartley Cooper and Co. While at the school Dancey turned from the piano to the organ and was taught by the Cathedral organist, rated as Europe's best in that era. And it was on St. Paul's glorious organ that Dancey played continually after hours and, as he liked to think, despite a Diocesan prohibition of such practices.

When the time came to bid adieu to the classroom and his childhood, Sir Ernest took Dancey aside.

"There is," he said, "a junior position ready for you in my firm. Let Lloyd's be your future. Follow music as an enchanting hobby but not as a source of bread and butter."

This offer and even the advice were accepted with gratitude. Time passed. Sir Ernest, pursuing his Aldermanic path towards the Mayoralty of London, found himself more and more frequently an honoured guest at the splendid dinners given by the various City Livery Companies. It was the custom at these functions for choristers to sing Grace before and after meat and sometimes medieval glees and catches while the Loving Cup went round. Sir Ernest, delighting in fine harmony, much enjoyed that delivered by a quartette, 'The Gresham Singers', who were newcomers on the civic scene. It was however with a vague discomfort that he ultimately recognised the leader of this group as Messrs. Hartley Cooper's Mr. A. H. Dancey, no longer a mere cipher in that important concern but an aide of standing. Here, he thought, was a situation not quite *comme il faut* and needing correction. One morning, with last night's chanted 'Amens' still ringing in his ears, Sir Ernest put his feelings to Dancey and suggested that the pre- and post-prandial choir work might be dropped.

"Why, of course, sir," replied Dancey, "if that is what you wish—but (sadly) I shall miss the money!"

"There will be a proper adjustment" was the answer "—and thanks, Dan!"

Long after this episode Dancey, now well established in the Box, one day sought leave to take his lunch-break an hour earlier than usual.

Francis agreed with a "Nothing serious I hope?"

"Not at all," said Dancey, "but a lot of my pals are going to an organ recital at St. Michael's, Cornhill."

"And you think you should join them?"

"Yes, I'd better (pause) I'm doing the playing!"

"When he told me of this," Francis said, "I had not the least idea at that time how highly gifted Dan was in this particular field", nor had his congregation of young friends (many living on a tight budget) the least idea that the recital would precede a silver collection. The 'take' was an offertory record. The Rector was delighted and booked Dan for a repeat performance. But once bitten twice shy! At Dan's next show his former audience, according to Francis' slightly coloured account, kept away and the pews were empty.

FOUR

F.R.B. ON LLOYD'S JAPES AND LEG-PULLS

IT must not be thought that the F.R.B. Box while unusual in the provenance of its occupants was also unique in sometimes handling serious business on a basis of levity. Indeed this attitude was common throughout the Room. It just happened that Francis, whom I met almost daily in the City or in our respective homes and who approached life with a rich appreciation of its funnier aspects, was the source from which I drew nearly all the yarns which in after years were to break into print. I believe the first story he told me was about a practical joke which must have been played in the very early nineteen hundreds. At any later period the City Police, with small sympathy for the so-called 'automobile' (nuisances which stank abominably and startled horses), would not have let a certain Lloyd's broker leave his scarlet, low-slung car against the kerb in Cornhill. Neither on the custom-built body nor on the radiator was there any sign to identify the car's maker. But curious pedestrians, including some bitten by the new craze for 'horseless carriages' saw that each hub cap wore a ring of lettering. To read this lettering one had to lower one's head nearly to pavement level. Many performed this gymnastic feat only to hurry away red-faced. The lettering read '*Nosey Parker*'. I would not say that Lloyd's jokes ran mainly to the practical; they often did and Francis himself was at times guilty of them. As World War I, which was expected to last only a few months, ran into its second and third year desperate efforts were made by brokers and underwriters to fill the places of their staff members who had gone into the

Armed Forces, many never to return. Few, if any of the newcomers had any previous insurance experience. But the old hands did all they could to show them the ropes and this in the friendliest and most informal way. One such replacement, let us call him Captain X, a young discharged veteran short of one eye 'showed' Francis a slip inviting insurance on some tuns of Oporto in warehouse. "This, of course," said Francis gravely, "will be subject to the Quill and Gimlet exclusion. I think I have a gummed print of it here." After raking through his desk drawer for this non-existent and sheer absurdity he added, "Sorry! No luck. But I'm sure Mr. Nicholls over there will oblige you with one." Hubert Augustus Nicholls (how he hated that 'Augustus'!) when asked for the clause kept a straight face (he was rather saturnine at the best) hunted through his drawer and, cursing Francis for not having a proper supply of forms on hand, told Captain X to get the Quill and Gimlet clause from his own office. This happened on a Friday. Francis in relating this leg-pull said, "It did not enter the poor chap's mind that the idea of anyone inserting a quill through a gimlet hole to steal port wine from a 250-gallon cask tottered on the verge of lunacy. I learned over the phone that he had been cruelly teased by his colleagues and that he was out for my blood. I also learned he had been welter-weight champion of his native Colony. So I took the Saturday off and Dug for Victory, giving him the week-end to cool down. He came to see me on the Monday using the most awful language and then howled with laughter. A good sort!" Anyone familiar with Lloyd's ways would know from the foregoing that Captain X must have been likeable and popular. Had he not been no one would have bothered to play such a trick on him at all.

It was inevitable and excusable that these newcomers while learning how Lloyd's ticks over would drop a few clangers. The F.R.B. Box did a fine business indemnifying gentlemen against the risk of their pregnant wives producing twins. I willingly believe that one ex-soldier turned broker's clerk, given the routine task of notifying clients that their insurances would shortly expire, had tactlessly invited renewal from an insured who had only a month earlier collected a 'total loss' under one of these 'twins' policies. But I regard as apocryphal a yarn about a man recently taken on by that greatly respected Brokerage house, Messrs. Leslie and Godwin. He had zealously studied all the Lloyd's forms he could lay his hands on and was much attracted by the Marine Policy which began, with medieval piety, 'In the Name of God. Amen'. He is said to have drafted a slip headed 'In the Name of Leslie and Godwin. Amen'.

My cousin-by-marriage, William Charles Campbell, and Francis had been office boys together at Hartley Cooper's. Their friendship was life-long and their Lloyd's adventures while differing in detail led each of them to the command of leading non-marine syndicates. Campbell and I were known to Francis a little indelicately as "The two W.C.s". But my thoughts turn to even a third 'W.C.', Colonel W. C. Bersey. This gentleman, ever ready to seize a promising opportunity, had introduced to London, as it transpired, before the streets were ready for them, the first electric cabs. Following distinguished service in the Air Force he launched and ran the "White Cross Motor Policies". When, as Lloyd's put it, "Peace broke out" in 1918 new cars were hard to come by. Bersey, always a jump ahead of the herd, obtained a contract from the Belgian manufacturers of the excellent sleeve valve 'Minerva' to supply him with I think fifty of their chassis for early delivery. He then sold off these chassis mostly to Lloyd's people. Francis and I were among his first customers.

Francis rejoiced in my expanding practice but, more for his own amusement than for the good of my soul, he would teasingly and without the least tinge of malice or substantial excuse deplore my alleged love of luxury. Dressed in his usual hodden-grey he attended meets of the West Kent Fox Hounds and grinned at me sitting on horseback wearing my red hunting coat. Yet he erected gates for me so that I might the more easily hack of a Sunday across country the five miles between my home and his. And he fixed up a small stable where the horses could rest in comfort while his wife, his adored 'Dinah', served our Sabbath elevenses. Nothing so far as he could avoid it, save perhaps his beautiful grounds, gave the least indication that he was a man of means. (He much relished being taken for his own gardener.) Nothing so far as I could avoid it was allowed to modify my luxurious enjoyment of things which I could at last afford.

It was therefore to be expected that his Minerva chassis when it reached England was sent to a local garage to be fitted with a modest nondescript open body painted in a flat neutral tint. Mine went to a swell firm almost in the Rolls-Royce class and emerged as a superb saloon affair enamelled in two shades of beige. My growing family excused the car's size and I still think Francis was wrong in believing it was often credited with belonging to the Buckingham Palace fleet.

* * *

A summer's day came when I was to drive this fine example of the coachbuilders' art down to Francis' Dymchurch beach house. We stopped in Ashford for morning coffee. My passengers, Francis and Vernon Wood, my partner, strolled off ostensibly in search of tobacco. When, after our coffee break, we continued our journey it was borne in on me that passers-by looking at our car found it not so much admirable as laughable. This was puzzling. But a glance at the back seat gave me the message. At Ashford

Francis and Vernon had bought not tobacco but gor'blimey Coster caps, red cotton chokers and clay pipes. Thus equipped they felt they were cutting my lordly Minerva (surely not me?) down to size. This leg-pull was typical not only of Francis but of Lloyd's attitude to fun in general. Wounding jokes were barred. A victim was never held up to lasting "hatred, ridicule and contempt", as the lawyers say. Those gently pilloried were almost exclusively likeable and popular types. There might be mild derision, perhaps a snub for the very few who committed the unforgivable sin of putting on side, e.g. the brainless Name with a perpetual itch to hint at his vast wealth, was guyed from time to time but no one bothered to slap him down hard. On the other hand there was nothing but a warm-hearted welcome for the broker whose conversation was adorned with side-splitting and absolutely unconsciously mangled metaphors, the best ever retailed being his blasting of a rival as 'a snake in the ointment'.

FIVE

THE HISTORY OF LLOYD'S LOG AND MY ANONYMOUS CONTRIBUTIONS

ON a May day in 1930 when eight Lloyd's Staff men were talking about their Sports Club and similar activities, one of them, to wit Edward G. Chapman, had an inspiration and made a resolution; "I shall start a Lloyd's Magazine!" said he. Now Fate in her wisdom had bestowed upon this young man (henceforth called "the Editor") the benefit of a singularly obstinate disposition. It need hardly be noted therefore that to his colleagues' hints of insanity and gloomy predictions that his project could neither be launched nor, if launched, kept afloat the Editor turned a stone-deaf ear. Forthwith he put the proposition to his Chief, the Principal Clerk, Mr. Thomas Devereux, whose zest for any new idea he judged worthy of support was notorious. In this instance he gave his blessing at once; "A Lloyd's Magazine? Right, laddie! Start small and build up. And find a name for it!" I have before me as I write No. 1 of this infant publication. Its date, 2nd June 1930, its size 7½″ × 5″, its contents three yellowish pages of sports fixtures and results, its modest title "Monthly Notes". The baby put on weight so fast that at two years old its girth ran to twelve pages. The time was ripe for a change. The Editor had long since felt it too much that production of this ever-growing bulk should remain a task for the small but willing staff of office duplicating machine operators. They must be relieved of these duties while he himself would like to bid adieu to the heavy collating and stapling job, one which took more of his evenings at home than he could reasonably be expected to spare.

Holding these views, and now that the demand for "Monthly Notes" had become manifest, he arranged for the mechanical production to be taken over by Lloyd's own fully-equipped printing department. At this stage it was felt that the publication, straying well beyond its original fields of athleticism and such, merited a new name, something terse but significant of its habitat and its aims. Born of the sea and still retaining a salty flavour, how could Lloyd's, thought the Editor, record the doings of its community more appropriately than in a 'LOG' just as ships had recorded their own doings ever since the fifteenth century? But unhappily this name, the ideal name, was found to be in use elsewhere. Here was a snag which called for rethinking. After much cogitation the trite title "Lloyd's Office Gazette" received approval. By the oddest coincidence the initial letters of this title spelled "L. O. G.". However no howls of protest came from anyone and at a date which I cannot specify, the coast was clear and the discreet full stops disappeared.

* * *

Up to the outbreak of war in 1939 the LOG drew most of its material from the Committee's clerical staff and from a few Lloyd's Agents. These sources were apt to shrink. Providentially in 1940 the Chairman asked that the magazine's pattern should be spread to cover the Room, the brokers, the brokers' staffs and anyone else who could reasonably be thought to come within Lloyd's orbit. By this timely expansion, one for which the Editor had always hoped, Lloyd's men on active service everywhere and many P.O.W.s bored nearly to despair were cheered with just the kind of news for which they hungered most, of what was going on in and about the Room, of its chameleon-like matching up to war conditions and, no doubt above all, of the promise that Lloyd's, physically intact and morally unbowed, would have their former places warm and waiting for them so soon as 'V' Day should provide them with the necessary return tickets. These messages struck home; a Naval Officer (ex-Lloyd's) from one of H.M.'s Cruisers at the request of his ward-room paid the Editor a visit especially to say so. This opening out of the LOG's coverage meant more editorial toil. The widening spheres of interest had to be explored for material of 'news value' in those areas. And if the magazine was to live up to its new shape as a full scale House Journal its pages must be enlivened by worthy illustrations. Good fortune helped in both respects. James Jarché, one of the leading Press photographers of the day, introduced his brother A. Louis Jarché, a man with outstanding professional skill, who was giving up Press photography for free-lance work. Skill alone was not enough; A.L.J. ("our" Jarché) to succeed as the pictorial recorder of Lloyd's daily life must have tact of a high order so that he could move around among underwriters and brokers as though invisible, accepted as bodies so rarely accept a transplant. He proved to have that tact in full measure and agreed, if at first a little reluctantly, to shoot what he was asked to shoot instead of shooting what he liked as he had done in the past. For seventeen eventful years his camera was in continual operation. His 2500 exposures perpetuate almost every conceivable Lloyd's happening, every picture a work of art and many of them—for example those of Lloyd's at War—of lasting historical importance.[1] The second piece of good fortune led the LOG into 'fresh woods and pastures new'. It came in the shape of George A. Deverell, alias 'Dev', of whom favourable mention was made in our earlier chapters. Grown up to be an Underwriting Member, a born mixer and immensely popular among his own generation, he had enthusiastically supported the LOG almost since its cradle

[1] See 'Lloyd's Under Fire. A tribute to the Civil Defence Services of Lloyd's—1938–1945' (Privately printed and published by Lloyd's, London).

days. In fact he was both Edward Chapman's close personal friend and his most fruitful liaison link with the Room. The magazine had been invited to spread its wings, 'Dev's' helpful efforts spread with them.

* * *

To browse through early copies of the LOG is, for an old 'un, a nostalgic exercise. One comes across reports of Art shows and Crafts contests (in some instances the first ever to be staged at Lloyd's) where Lloyd's people competed with one another in their hobbies all the way from the purl and plain of knitting to the deft brushwork of impressive but not impressionistic painting. There are crosswords and there are puzzles. And in 1942 Mr. W. G. Gooda, the well-known Marine Underwriter who enjoys mathematics to the nth degree, sent in the first of a series of simple looking but treacherous 'Problems'. They were to appear continually for twenty-seven years. Many were solvable by ordinary readers unblessed by the Gooda-type mind; others required some familiarity with 'those damned dots' of the Decimal System or worse. But many poor souls bearing one of war's bitterest inflictions, sheer boredom, looked forward eagerly to this monthly anodyne. To satisfy their craving Mr. Gooda, in March 1944, agreed to compile 250 specimens for a 'Lloyd's LOG Problem Book'. Decorated with cheerful little black-and-white sketches and given only a stingy fourteen blank pages for 'trial and error working out' (250 would have been nearer my mark) it was comfortably tailored to fit the standard uniform tunic pocket. The first consignment went to Lloyd's own P.O.W.s; then, to reach the Forces in general, some three thousand were put on sale through the Railway Book stalls and sold like hot cakes. Did the troops like them? Let us by way of answer quote one man who came back to Lloyd's after the Allied Landings. "When we were dug in on Anzio Beach," he said, "I wanted to take my mind off the murderous fire which was pinning us down. Suddenly I remembered my LOG Problem Book so I pulled it out and set to. It was a Godsend!" We may well wonder which of the brain twisters wooed him to forgetfulness of his mortal peril. Was it the Story of the Secretive Hen who, plus half a hen, laid an egg and a half in a day and a half but would not disclose how many eggs six of them could lay in a week?; or did he require stronger medicine, something with square roots and trigonometric scales in it?

* * *

The war had been going for two years when 'Dev', always out to recruit LOG contributors, asked me if I would write down some of F.R.B.'s favourite Lloyd's yarns with which we were both familiar? F.R.B. was in on this approach and ready to give me comprehensive notes so that, as he said, I would only have to 'ghost' his stuff. Thus began the 'Once upon a time' stories which I wrote anonymously for 'Dev' to hand along. In spite of severe paper rationing the editor found room and continued to find room for these authentic Historical Essays feeling that they afforded a little light relief in the rather depressing days through which we were passing.[1] I disinter, enlarge upon and incorporate the essays in these my Reminiscences hoping first that the post-war LOG readers to whom they are unfamiliar may be amused to read of their predecessors' goings-on and secondly in the

[1] In 1945 the burden of Edward G. Chapman's official duties forced him to leave the editorship in other hands, he regained overall responsibility for Lloyd's Log from 1948–1961; during this period he was responsible for Lloyd's press and public relations as well as the Corporation's extensive premises.

On his retirement in 1961 after 44 years' service Lloyd's Log published an appreciation in which some of his outstanding achievements and creations for Lloyd's (e.g. The Information Department (1948) under whose aegis the LOG is published) received honourable mention.

hope that some modern F.R.B. will be prompted to do as he did, jot down accounts of Lloyd's current japes and leg-pulls lest they fade from memory for ever. There was much sagacity in Cap'n Cuttle's advice 'when found make a note of'.

* * *

The LOG has never lost the top rating it scored among Press critics and professional editors of House magazines while still under Edward G. Chapman's direction. The present make-up, that of a profusely illustrated 'glossy' with a nine thousand circulation adheres *mutatis mutandis* to its World War II image, that of a true House Journal picturing for Lloyd's multifarious contracts every angle of their doings and concerns in every corner of the globe.

SIX

WILLIAM SHAKESPEARE AND THE BOER WAR

THE first yarn which I chose from F.R.B.'s wide repertoire for submission to the LOG editor took one back to the Boer War. Afrikaans farmers with their unsporting introduction of a new military weapon, i.e. barbed wire, and the much too accurate use of their sporting rifles, put our own traditional troops to gravely embarrassing disadvantages. Moreover, hordes of indigenous bacilli grappling in vain to prosper despite the immunity built up by the locals turned with relief and relish to the thick blood of the British invaders and took a heavy toll. Against these obstacles, the wire, disease, superiority of marksmanship, mobility and dare we say superior and imaginative leadership, our army met initially a series of pride-shattering defeats. It was obvious to every Briton that this distressing situation screamed aloud for a doubling or trebling of our forces. As usual in such emergencies the necessary enlargement came from the picked youth among the civil population. The City of London may be said to have set the example with their new-formed City Imperial Volunteers or for short 'The C.I.V.s'. Those of us who have lived long enough will recall the unusual head-dress with which they were adorned; a distant cousin of the Stetson, it had a low crown dented in and a wide brim turned up vertically over the left ear. Westminster street cleaners wore similar hats and the Aussies have immortalized the style in subsequent wars. The C.I.V.s were a gallant carefree lot; moreover, they ran to occasional jokes as

F.R.B.'s story will show. It appeared in the LOG during World War II and ran as follows:

ONCE UPON A TIME—to wit, many years ago—there was an Underwriter—a Most Distinguished Underwriter—whose business methods were scrupulously correct. If he had possessed a sense of humour he would have been blessed with all the virtues. His policies, in accordance with the practice of those distant days, were signed in the Room by two clerks, one of whom, alas, suddenly found himself under a month's notice. The clerk in question (let us call him John Brown), in common with his distinguished employer, had himself never evinced the faintest humorous tendency, perhaps because the signing of hundreds of policies day after day, month after month, "per pro John Brown" was singularly lacking in comicality, or, perhaps, with the knowledge that any manifestations in lighter vein would have hastened the bestowal of the sack. Though outwardly and visibly the same, John Brown —as we insist on calling him —during the last of those thirty glorious days of his service suffered a sea change rich and whimsical. John Brown, it may be said, just disappeared, but strange and famous persons took possession of his mortal body. His policies were, in consequence, signed by no less a celebrity than Dan Leno, more by Henry Irving, by Gus Elen and Albert Chevalier. And when apparently these gentlemen relinquished their clerical duties, Julius Caesar himself returned from the Shades for one busy period, during which he undoubtedly signed more policies than he had subscribed throughout the whole of his earthly and Imperial career. Strange to relate, the presence of these immortals passed without a soul noticing, or, at least, reporting anything unusual, until, after the clerk had departed, a Broker of impressive mien, monocled, outraged, menacing but still dignified, approached this Most Distinguished and Correct of Underwriters flourishing half-a-dozen policies and demanding to know whether the individual who had signed them was, in fact and in law, qualified to sign himself "W. Shakespeare", or whether the incredible had happened and someone was trying to be funny. And before many more hours had elapsed, other Brokers visited the Box seeking the honour of a personal introduction to the clerk who was sometimes Dan Leno and sometimes Julius Caesar, but they were doomed to disappointment, for that protean performer, clothed in khaki and wearing an unusual hat, was on his way to South Africa as a C.I.V. to fight in the war before last.

SEVEN

ONE SUCH RELATED—CHARLES GOULD ON CARTHAGE

ONE thing of which there can be small doubt is that in a country at war grand pianos are hard to sell. In September 1914 a lad who had been at work in that field opted for the Army. Two years later he came home badly beaten up. Six months in hospital did all that could be done to give a maimed left hand some but not much of its past dexterity. While the call for grand pianos was by then as dead as Queen Anne the call for young men with brains and "Unfit" only in a military sense was endless. Charles Gould, pining for work, had the good luck to drop into a job with a strong go-ahead Brokerage house at Lloyd's. At that time all he knew of insurance could have been set out in a fair round hand on half a sheet of note paper. But his luck held. William Charles Campbell (my fellow 'W.C.') never forgot the pangs of shyness which wracked him when as a callow youth he had to find out for himself how the Room functioned. The leg-pulls invited by that shyness he misinterpreted as snubs and he suffered the more. For the rest of his life he went out of his way by hints and quiet correction to steer any such neophyte as he had been along the right Lloyd's path. Francis Bussell, hag-ridden by no such sore memories, kind and generous beyond belief, tendered (anonymously if that could be) help to any who might want it. To these two able men Charles found he could turn whenever he encountered problems. No one could have had abler mentors and no mentors a more apt and able pupil.

One must not think that 'W.C.' or Francis came the pedagogue in what today would be called their 'communication' with Charles. Far from it. He and Francis became warm friends; they took morning coffee together in a Telegraph Street dive frequently with me one of the party. Now and then Francis would bring out a few slips from his coat pocket—"He carries them about like that until the ink fades," said Charles. These were discussed in lighter and maybe defamatory vein. I do not doubt that Francis's sage advice usually emerged from the gentle raillery in which he habitually indulged. If one of the slips was drawn in words so few as to raise the thought that they might fall short of the whole truth Francis would let me say my piece on it; that an Insurance Contract, being in Law a contract *Uberimmæ Fidei*, i.e. one demanding between the parties the utmost good faith, a policy is voidable if obtained by concealment from the underwriter of facts material for him to know in weighing the risk. After me Francis would take up the theme in his own words and these after a lapse of sixty years can but echo in my memory as a paraphrase, to wit:

"William Charles' 'you bury me if I die' stuff is, we may be sure, the real McCoy. But the guts of the matter can be put quite simply in English. A broker, for example you Charles, may go short on the damning facts, and sell me as 'Jam' a risk that he well knows is a stinker. He picks me up in this sly manner once or twice. But never again! He has lost for the sake of pleasing a client or two his most precious asset, his reputation. Let him tell me more than is relevant if he wishes to, but if he tells me less, then we part brass-rags."

Francis would assume an 'I have spoken' look. Charles would give a solemn nod of deferential acquiescence. Each of course was gently ribbing the other. And to illustrate that such was common practice between them, here is the story I ghosted for Francis in the August 1941 LOG.

ONCE UPON A TIME or to be precise one hundred and forty-six years before the Christian Era one Scipio Aemilianus Africanus let loose his Roman legionaries to plunder and burn the defeated city of Carthage; moreover he forbade all human habitation throughout the ruined area and with appropriate ceremonial dedicated it to the infernal gods. The spell so cast upon the evil spot, it was said, meant certain death to any who should so much as dare to ruffle its dust or pile one Carthaginian stone upon another; nor it would seem did this magic grow less lethal as the centuries rolled by and from first to last the list of those impelled by vanity, curiosity, ambition, the lust for knowledge, or what you will, who rooted among the rubble and then met their respective and untimely ends was a long and impressive one.

But the hungry mind of man (and woman) is insatiable and all the dire experience of the past was swept aside as of naught when a famous Ladies' College in the U.S.A., seeking the archaeological low-down on Scipio and his fell work, subsidised an expedition, not of mere dust rufflers but of hefty Poles who were to descend upon the forbidden scene with pick and shovel and thereafter cross the Atlantic to lecture upon their finds. It was, of course, a rash and hazardous undertaking, predestined only to promote the business of the Funeral Furnisher. Successively but inescapably the learned excavators mysteriously died until, with the inevitability of gradualness which had afflicted the Ten Little Nigger Boys, only one was left to attempt the necessary voyage to the States. Was there a hope that he would ever see the Ambrose Light?—and if so, could he then expect to make the final grade from the Cunard Pier to the University Hall where sophomores and so on would parade, gaily attired and ready with orations in the various dead tongues?

The need for a Lloyd's Accident Policy (technically 'K.5' but colloquially 'Death and Spare Parts') was obvious but where could be found a broker—courageous, silver-tongued, magnetic and compelling—to place such a risk? And where could be found the underwriter willing to consider it at less than £125 per cent?

It has well been said that the Hour produces the Man; in this particular instance it produced two. On the one hand a young broker with all the qualities and on the other a young underwriter whose enterprise in unfamiliar insurance fields had already crowned him with the gilded laurels of the pioneer. "This," said the former fluttering his slip hypnotically, "is the veritable Plum and Apple—and for information I hand you the disastrous story of two thousand years with amusing speculations on a variety of corpses. Read it at your leisure and if you feel inclined to cut the normal 150s. rate, just for a lark, my lips shall be sealed." In the result the rate was neither cut nor increased. That the broker's skill would produce a quote of some sort was a foregone conclusion, that he would secure a premium reduction was more than even his own especial brand of optimism might contemplate; nevertheless he had his reward in an unique extension of cover for the slip was returned marked "150s. per cent. including Cursing". And for those who like happy endings we have to record that the Professor was an "arrival".

EIGHT

F.R.B. ON HIS FATHER'S CLERK

FRANCIS disliked what he called 'lawyers' jargon'. "When," said he, "I have more or less agreed with a broker some novel risk 'in the round' as it were and you have the simple task of putting it down in words please cut out the 'whereases' and the 'hereinbeforesaids'; aim at language brief and so clear that even the assured can grasp what it means."

"Why do you think," said I, "that the archaic marine policy wording goes unchanged from generation to generation? Not for love of tradition nor out of respect for the Shade of Edward Lloyd but because its every phrase, over the years, has been the subject of litigation wherein the courts have given those phrases precise definition. No draughtsman unless he is a fathead thinks up words of his own when he has legally defined ones ready to hand. These 'precedents' are the crutches which afford the good lawyer support when he has to wend his way through the Law's dark jungles. We lack precedents enough to fit your pioneering projects. One of the risks you run is that if some day a disgruntled claimant sues you the learned judge may hold that our words which we meant to mean 'chalk' in the eyes of the Law meant 'cheese'. Problems of this sort arise from your urge to fit new ideas to the New Age scorning the example of your revered father, that ultra-conservative underwriter who would have recoiled in horror had the least deviation from time-honoured insurance practice been proposed to him."

"You may be right about me," Francis replied, "but you are wrong about my father. He was no stick-in-the-mud; he was an innovator and invented the 'T.L.O.'—Total Loss Only—policy. Moreover he was very human and knew how to hold his tongue."

As evidence of this latter virtue Francis gave me the story which I wrote up for the LOG of March 1943.

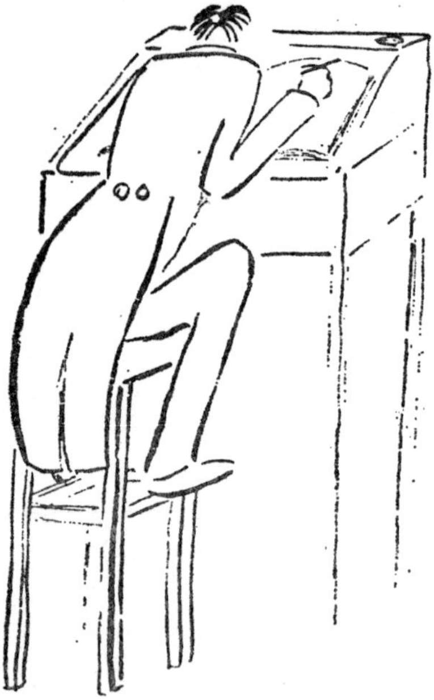

ONCE UPON A TIME there was a young man named Hugh Stowell Scott who aspired to become a novelist. But his father, a City merchant and a Name on Lloyd's, would hear naught of such folly.

"The good friend who underwrites for me," said he, "is most courteously finding you a post in his office, and there you will ply your pen to real purpose. Say no more to me about writing books!"

"Very well, sir," replied the son, "I won't!"

And so Hugh, obedient to the parental command, resigned himself philosophically to the circumstances. Moreover, he made a good clerk. And a happy one at that, since every moment he could spare from the letters and ledgers of his unwanted calling was secretly devoted to the scribbling of romantic stories.

They were good stories; so good that publishers took them and sold them by the thousand.

They were indeed so superlatively good that Mr. Scott senior, himself an omnivorous reader, devoured them with avidity, quite unconscious of the fact that his son was their creator.

"How willingly, Hugh," said that worthy merchant, "would I have agreed your choice of profession if you could have produced tales like these!"

Hugh, safe behind his *nom de plume*, smiled grimly, but made no reply. Had he not promised his father never to refer to that particular subject again?

Sad to relate, the old gentleman was allowed to die without enlightenment. In this respect some may think Hugh was a little hard, especially since his tolerant employer had been allowed to share the secret from the start, and treasured to the end of his days a complete set of his clerk's works inscribed by their author, in a fair hand:—

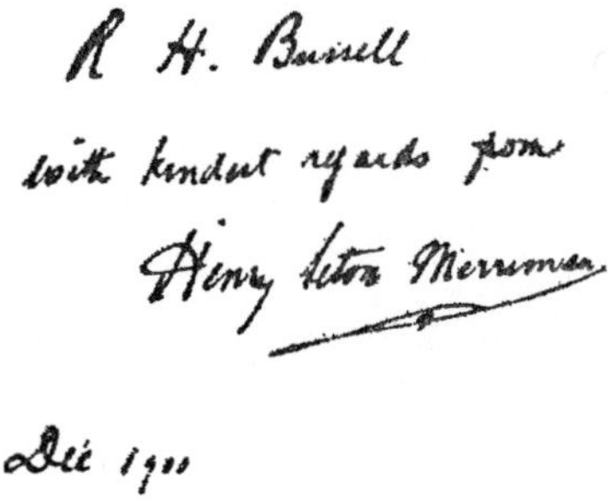

NINE

ON LLOYD'S HEAD-COLDS AND THE 1914 MUMPS

IN the year 1914 Lloyd's was struck by Plague, unheralded, long drawn out and fraught with pain. None could have predicted its coming. Science tardily put the blame for the Black Death on rats' fleas. Mosquitoes and other bugs were found guilty in respect of other lethal fevers. However my duty as an historian is to tell it as it was. The blame for the 1914 Plague falls not on entomology but plumb on the Committee. They had resolved that the Room's lino, clear wore out, must be scrapped. Thick, soft treading, sound deadening Para rubber should take its place. This was a welcome idea. But such is life, there was a hefty snag to it. Lloyd's could not shut up shop during the change-over. The Lloyd's men and the floor men, avoiding one another as much as possible, would have to rub along together as best they could. And thus the job went ahead. Up came the aged lino, section by section, and one by one and two by two and then in droves down went the Room's *habitués* with a low debilitating ailment. The salivary glands were swollen and tender; swallowing was a torture. Harley Street diagnosed the disease as *epidemic parotitis*. Family doctors called it Mumps. And since each fresh outbreak followed close on the heels of each fresh uprooting of lino it became obvious that thereunder lurked the filterable virus whose sole ambition is to promote this particular form of glandular grief. Nature, we maintain, is meant to inflict this disease only on the young, those of nursery age or little older. A grown man with mumps, his jowls puffed out grotesquely from ear to ear looks and feels ridiculous. Moreover if he tries an apologetic laugh his neck glands rebel instantly and crack with indescribable anguish. Full of sympathy as one may be his face contorted by the agony which wipes out the incipient grin is—and even the smitten victim wryly admits it—mirth-provoking in the extreme. And Lloyd's being Lloyd's therefore decided to treat the Visitation as a Heaven-sent practical joke. A small group of underwriters formed a select Market in which any Lloyd's adult could obtain cover to pay an agreed sum by way of total loss should he contract mumps within the year. It is said there was also under-the-counter betting. Lists of say thirty 'runners' for each race were compiled. Among these 'runners' the younger men, the likeliest to succumb, were 'favourites' and quoted accordingly at short odds; the elderly, probably immune and therefore classed as 'outsiders', were on offer at tempting prices. The first 'runner' in each event to fall sick would be declared the winner. Books were made, slips were passed, and in general the transactions (limited to shillings) displayed a dignified formality which would have been thought excessive for Ascot on Gold Cup Day. But behind this façade of fun and games lurked the grim fact that going down with mumps meant a week's painful misery and three weeks more of isolation as an infectious carrier. And there were superstitions: nobody has mumps twice. And an attack, must, alas, destroy a male's fertility? True or False? The answer is 'False' in both cases. I fell a victim to the Lloyd's epidemic towards its end having recovered from a previous attack some twenty years earlier, and four of my children were born long after that second attack had faded into the past.

* * *

The hygienically washed marble of the new Lloyd's Room, the purified air pumped in for pampered members to breathe, and the hermetically sealed windows eliminating draughts no doubt make it hard for bacilli and maybe even for the filterable lino-haunting virus to enter in. The head cold, although checked by hypodermic shots and antibiotics, is still with us if rarely in chronic year-round form. It must therefore be conceded that the following stories which I wrote for the LOG in March 1942 and June 1943 have become period pieces and in that guise are now resurrected.

ONCE UPON A TIME when Lloyd's was housed in the Royal Exchange, there was an Underwriter who sat next to one of the windows which looked down into the covered courtyard.

This suited him admirably, for he loved fresh air. He would have kept the window permanently open but for one unfortunate circumstance; a Member in the adjoining Box was in the highest degree susceptible to draughts.

Accordingly, when No. 1 raised the window No. 2 raised his collar in reproach and then had the offending window shut. What to No. 1 were "sweet airs, that give delight and hurt not" to No. 2 were harbingers of coughs and sneezes.

Inevitably a feud developed; literally "an up and a downer". It was waged with gentlemanly determination and its crisis came on a crisp spring morning. Anticipating the customary opposition from his neighbour No. 1 requested Mr. Jack Smith, the genial and diplomatic Superintendent of the Room, to lift the sash six inches. No. 2 sent for a waiter and had it shut. No. 1 sent for another waiter and had it reopened. He then strode across to his apparently frost-bitten foe and reasoned with him. He pointed out that, as the courtyard was entirely roofed in, it was scientifically incapable of emitting anything even remotely resembling a draught; that, indeed, No. 2 would do well to conquer delusions and phobias of this kind; and might make a good start by trying to appreciate that until the Laws of Nature should be suspended no draught would ever flow from this particular orifice.

Thus addressed, No. 2 regarded No. 1 coldly, drew himself up to his full height and marched purposefully out of the Room. But not in defeat: his retirement was manifestly strategic, a mere deployment in good order, *reculer pour mieux sauter*. Sure enough twenty minutes later he returned carrying one of the little coloured paper windmills, which, in those unsophisticated days, were sold by the thousand for the amusement of the young.

He contrived to plant this in the window opening: without a word to anyone, he resumed his seat.

No. 1's eyes fixed themselves in fascinated embarrassment upon the toy; its tiny sails revolved furiously like a sparkless but colourful Catherine Wheel, affording a perfect example of a beautiful Theory shattered in collision with a brutal Fact.

As Old Kaspar said on another occasion, " 'Twas a famous victory."

Once Upon A Time *O Tempora! O Mores!*—in that coloured era which we call the 'Nineties, there was an elderly, unmarried, Underwriting Member of Lloyd's (shall we call him Bernard?) who manifested two strong idiosyncracies. He was extremely susceptible to colds in the head, and he entertained a low submissive reverence for the Gentler Sex.

At the merest suspicion of a draught his nose would take an azure tinge as though that organ had been Red Litmus and the air current assailing it, strongly Alkaline. Constantly alive to the evil propensities of treacherous winds he went about for ever well defended, his coat collar snugly raised, and a silken topper thrust well down upon his crown.

Thus armed against the perils of catarrh he left his Box whenever duty badc him brave the insidious breezes of the open streets; outwardly, sedate and circumspect but inwardly and spiritually, jousting in the Lists of Chivalry.

For above all he was chivalrous; and from the depths of his admiration for Woman in the Abstract there flowed the sense of personal unworthiness which doomed him to a life-long, if happy, celibacy.

Came a day of icy blasts when he was encountered straying from his Box bareheaded. Such a phenomenon could have been matched only by the advent of a beardless Farrant! One almost expected the Lutine Bell to sound the tocsin!

A friend in the Gangway (Harrison will do for a name) challenged his hatless state and asked with great concern, "No hat! Will you not catch your death?"

Bernard scanned the quarter-acre floor of Lloyd's in a backward sweeping glance, much as the Ancient Marincr, in dcspair, swept the waste of waters in hope of a passing ship.

"They tell me, Harrison," he whispered, "there is a

Lady somewhere in the Room!"

And then with reverential tread and stately mien he made his way, his headgear primly perched upon his wrist, as Quixote might have dipped his plumed casque in honour of the Fair Dulcinea.

And this was scarcely fifty years ago. O parfit gentil knight! O Shades of Bayard and Du Guesclin! O Galahad! *O* (we repeat) *Tempora! O Mores!*

TEN

THE CALLER WALTER FARRANT—GUIDE, PHILOSOPHER AND FRIEND

THE honour of being the first to act as 'caller' at Lloyd's goes to a boy. He was a boy on the staff of Lloyd's Coffee House in Tower Street, E.C., *circa* 1685. For some long lost reason he went by an odd sobriquet 'The Kidney'. His main duty was to read aloud to the customers the latest shipping news which the runners, employed by his farsighted master, Edward Lloyd, had pried out of sailors and such along the Thames-side docks and wharves. If apart from this broadcasting he also obliged the customers by accepting and passing on messages among them from one to the other he thus laid down in broad outline a routine for all the Lloyd's callers who were to succeed him during the next two hundred and fifty years. This routine, however, had to march with the times. As early as 1696 the word-of-mouth delivery of news met a strong rival when Edward Lloyd began the issue of a thrice-weekly printed News Sheet, the embryo of today's *Lloyd's List*. In effect this took over the work of the caller so far as general news went; he was left to deal only with any urgent news items which might suddenly crop up. But his usefulness remained. The Coffee House clientele—the 'Regulars' (later to be styled 'Members')—rapidly increased in number. The caller, always on the spot, became more and more valuable to them as a convenient channel through which they could reach one another. In 1774 when the upper floor of the Royal Exchange was fitted out (of course on Coffee House lines), to be Lloyd's home for a century and a half, the caller, in order that he might function the better, was given a nautical speaking trumpet, predecessor of the megaphone. No ordinary voice could have made itself heard in every corner of the Room's wide area without it.

The Committee of Lloyd's were troubled when in 1879 a new caller was needed. Where could they hope to find the ideal man, one with three essential gifts; a phenomenal voice, a fine memory and a naturally polite mien which would command the Room's respect? This apparently insoluble problem solved itself in the most improbable way. A Member of the Committee, passing in his train through Windsor Station, noticed a tall young bearded porter who was singing out strongly, clearly and most attractively the names of the stations ahead. In a moment of inspiration the Member beckoned the porter over and asked him to come to Lloyd's for an interview if he wanted a better job. That porter was Walter Farrant, endowed by nature in the highest degree with voice, mind and presence and ordained thereby to become the most famous caller Lloyd's was ever to have. His memory and wonderfully resonant tones were fabulous. Within a short time of his appointment he knew every underwriter and broker and their deputies by name and sight. Hour after hour tirelessly and using no amplifying device whatever he sang out calls for those of them who were wanted at the Rostrum to meet the person who had put in the call or to receive a message ("A Mr. Smith at the barrier for you, sir"). For each individual he had a special melody which he used for nobody else. The individuals so favoured, it is said, grew unaware of other calls and heard only their own. He heralded announcements about overdue ships and other matters of general concern by ringing a small handbell.[1] When failing health forced his retirement in 1913 he was justly lauded as having achieved distinction in two separate fields; firstly as Lloyd's celebrated caller and

[1] It was not until 1897 that the Lutine Bell came from the Committee Room to hang in its present wrought-iron frame next to the Rostrum.

secondly as the City of London's most famous Toastmaster. The *Daily Mail* in their tribute to him and in comparing these two roles said, "It was in his more glorious and ceremonial aspect of Toastmaster that his genius shone most resplendently. At a great and stately banquet he was the very personification of its stateliness. The exaltation of his dignity exalted the occasion. A thousand years of splendid tradition were in his bearing and reached the supreme moment of culminating triumph when his vibrant voice rose and rumbled among the rafters. No one without a thrill heard for the first time his noble declamation of the famous speech 'My Lords and Gentlemen! Be pleased to charge your glasses! And give silence for your chairman! The Right Honourable the Lord Mayor of London!'

With what scornful incredulity in the far-off Windsor Station days would not the young porter have dismissed a prediction that a new, prosperous and distinguished life lay ahead of him, that Lloyd's men by the thousand would be his admiring friends, that City of London Livery Companies would vie with one another for his services and that he would be privileged to have speech with his own Monarch and with nearly all the other contemporary crowned heads of Europe.

* * *

Walter Farrant was a Devonian. Those of us who hail from the County of Devon have been heard to admit that there is none better. The son of Robert Farrant, a gardener, Walter was born in the family home 'Cotford' at Sidbury, Sidmouth, on 17th November 1853. No doubt he mastered the 'Three Rs' in the Village School and then quit to go to work so soon as the law allowed. When at age twenty-five Lloyd's rescued him he was doing well as a full-fledged porter. That he and his mates had to shout out station names was an unimportant almost negligible part of the daily round. It was brawn and the easy ability to heave luggage that made Walter worth his salt. This particular porter's golden voice had in all probability gone wholly disregarded; a Caruso playing scene-shifter! It is certain that in a remarkably short time after his start at Lloyd's on 1st July 1879 the outstanding character of this new bearded caller became apparent. With a quiet native dignity he gave all and earned from all a proper degree of respect. His sense of justice was legendary. No one could jump the queue of those waiting to put in a call. The most senior Member trying it on would be told, "The lad is ahead of you, sir!" His all-round worth to brokers and underwriters alike, F.R.B. told me, resulted in Christmas Boxes thought, in total, to double or treble his substantial salary. Self-taught except for his village schooling he had, like so many of his kind, done well by his own teaching. He was never facetious, he never played for laughs. His real wit was shown when a lady asked him, "But what *is* Lloyd's?" "Madam," he replied, "individually we are underwriters; collectively we are Lloyd's." It is claimed that 'As a succinct definition this cannot be bettered'.[1]

* * *

His final day at Lloyd's, 30th May 1913, he took in his stride bravely and with no sign of emotion. There were Presentations in the Committee Room, an illuminated Address, a handsome clock, cheques totalling £550, a Bonus of undisclosed value and he was told his pension would be £220 a year for life. He gave thanks and returned to the Rostrum. There, obtaining silence by ringing the Lutine Bell, he 'called' his thanks in a joyful tone as though reporting the safety of an overdue ship. His words were "Gentlemen, the 'Annuity' has arrived A.1.". At 4 p.m. he stepped

[1] In 'The History of Lloyd's' by Wright and Fayle.

down to the floor and stood at attention for all his friends, the brokers and underwriters and their deputies to file past and shake his hand and wish him many happy carefree days in his Devon home. Poor brave Walter Farrant knew he could look forward to nothing but an early death; the 'ill-health' that forced his retirement was diabetes, a disease which in those pre-Insulin days was incurable. With thoughts of Probate Duty in mind he characteristically arranged his affairs accordingly. When he died nearly two years later his Estate left (save for specific legacies worth perhaps £150) wholly to his wife, was proved at only £880. His widow lived on until 1939 and left what Walter, one may fairly assume, had given her in expectation of his coming end, just on £7,000.

* * *

F.R.B. had many tales of this remarkable man but the yarn he and 'Dev' encouraged me to write for the LOG in November 1941 ran as follows:

ONCE UPON A TIME nearly half a century ago, waiters, laden with the statelier dailies and the weekly pictorials, made their morning rounds of the Room catering for the journalistic and literary appetites of individual underwriters; leisure for perusal seemed never lacking, and no broker alive to his own interests would dream of interrupting these matutinal browsings by the presentation of a sticky risk. Life was then indeed an idyll: business knew its proper place. The Underwriting Members even boasted a gifted few—maybe a dozen—who year in and year out never wrote a single risk, had no staff, no books, no office and yet, by some process the secret of which has, alas, been lost, managed to keep their Names sweet and contented. Among these Lotus eaters was one—let us call him Gristham—who, having married money in the most liberal interpretation of that term, was consumed by anxiety lest any should be left unaware of his auriferous distinction. A ripple of pure delight ran through Lloyd's when he mentioned loftily that his daughters, under the tutelage of one of his footmen, were learning to ride the new safety bicycle "round the wine cellars", but when he conceived the idea of displaying at his Box vast bouquets of orchids and hot-house carnations in competition with the customary and modest jars of garden flowers which decorated the neighbouring tables the inevitable Joker of that period (and Lloyd's from Angerstein to Pulbrook has never been without one) decided the time was ripe for a lesson. Mr. Gristham was called to the telephone, which meant that he made the long pilgrimage from his seat to one of the two telephone booths recently installed by a revolutionary Committee in the lobby outside the Reading Room. His journey was in vain; he was not wanted after all. Returning to his Box he saw that in his absence the orchids and carnations had been whisked away and in their place leering at him there stood an enormous cauliflower with a label proudly proclaiming that it had gained for Mr. G. a First Prize at the Streatham Dog Show. His complexion chameleon-like assumed the greenery-yallery hue of the cauliflower itself, his already offended dignity blazed into a berserk fury and, hurling the vulgar vegetable to the ground, he executed a frantic war dance upon it and then, exhausted by this emotional outburst, fainted clean away. Amusement turned to alarm, but the watchful Farrant—most famous of all Lloyd's callers, aloft in his rostrum exercised a general vigilance over the Room and was ever ready for such an emergency. He dashed forward, and tucking G. under his powerful arm made for the window and waved the inanimate form in the breeze a hundred feet above the pavement until consciousness returned. Though not to be found in the text books, this was Farrant's invariable treatment for 'fits and faints'. Its unbroken success being largely due to the providential circumstance that he never lost his grip.

Moral: "Pride goeth before destruction."

ELEVEN

THE STORY OF AN OBSTINATE MAN

THOSE of us who were of school age in 1901 can still bring back to mind the real grief which was felt by all, high and low, when the Great Queen died in the first month of that year. Everyone who could went into deep mourning; those who could not wore at least a black tie or an armband. Even the ragged did so, the cab-runners, the crossing-sweepers, the down-and-outs. It would not be far from the truth if one said that the British Empire seemed to grind to a halt. It is against such a background of death and gloom and *pompes funèbres* that Francis' story of The Obstinate Man of Principle which I wrote for the July 1941 LOG should be read.

ONCE UPON A TIME on the 22nd January 1901, Victoria Regina et Imperatrix, Ruler and Symbol of the British Empire, wearily laid down the Royal Sceptre which she had so worthily wielded for sixty-four years and passed peacefully away. Nobody much under ninety could boast of remembering her birth; only septuagenarians could recall her Coronation. The vast majority of her subjects had been born as such. She had lifted Monarchy from odium to adoration, and when she died there was an incalculable and overwhelming sense not only that a Great Personality had left the stage, but that an Era had reached its end.

Manifestations of sorrow were universal; on all sides, either actually or figuratively, shutters went up in sign of mourning and there can be small doubt that the Room would have followed suit but for the inconvenient circumstance that the Charter governing Lloyd's in those days made no provision for such a contingency.

Here was a dilemma; to close down, however meritorious and desirable that might be, would involve illegality; to continue would be repugnant to those loyal sentiments which have ever animated this ancient institution. What was to be done?

Nelson, Lloyd's own especial hero, when faced with an order which he judged irreconcilable with the conditions of the moment, avoided inconvenience by putting a blind eye to his telescope. Mr. S. I. da Costa, similarly inspired on this fateful day, mounted the Rostrum with a metaphorical telescope under his arm and one eyelid lowered.

"Gentlemen," he said, in effect, "while it is true that an official resolution to close the Room would be *ultra vires,* we can achieve our respectful object by the simple process of all going home. If a broker carelessly ignores a client's instructions to insure a ship and the vessel is lost that broker may well expect to be sued for negligence, but it would be a complete answer for him if he could say that there was no underwriter available to look at the business. Hence the need for unanimity. Are we of one mind? Are we prepared to go home to a man?"

There was a roar of approval broken only by one dissentient voice, that of a rugged individualist, a stern upholder of Victorian principles, determined that so far as he was concerned the Charter should be honoured both in the letter and the spirit. He would occupy his Box as usual.

And so he sat from 11 a.m. to 4 p.m. dour and dignified and perhaps in himself a fitting monument to the character and solidity of the age whose knell was even then a-tolling; some such thoughts may have crossed the minds of those who by reason of his presence perforce remained with him in the theoretically open Room to represent brokerage firms and to keep faith with potential insurers in what for all practical purposes proved to be an absolutely idle market. On the other hand, their not unnatural irritation at being 'kept in' may have blinded them to the dramatic significance of the gesture, and some support for that view is to be found in the only slip which, History relates, was shown to the underwriter in question during his watch; it related to "Water in Paper Bags—With Average".

TWELVE

GOSS, THE DIMINUTIVE SPECIAL CONSTABLE

ONE could often pick up odd but useful facts at Lloyd's. Motor claims, for example, taught me that a tall driver has no more elevated a view than a short one since all our eyes, when we sit, are more or less on the same level. Nature has decreed that by and large human spines are roughly of equal length; height results in the main from the length of one's legs, not from that of the torso. Darling L.J., rightly famed for his sparkling wit and urbanity, always appeared in his caricatures as a distinctly diminutive person. Yet on the Appeal Court Bench there was little if anything to show that he was any smaller than the two other judges sitting with him. But artistically the caricaturists were not far from the truth. This I realised when his lordship came to me for professional help on behalf of his daughter who had been blamelessly involved in a fatal road collision. What modesty and charm he had and how easily one could forget his striking lack of inches and the fact that in occupying my clients' chair his feet barely touched the floor! On his death, years later, the Bar met to consider a proposition that a monument should be erected to his memory and to decide what form it should take. Theo Matthew, the Bar's genial satirist, asked 'Why not a life-sized statuette?' Darling L.J. would have loved that crack, one well in tune with his own genre.

And Lloyd's could boast a 'living statuette' to match him, my long time and esteemed friend Goss of Godsal's. A man of many talents, he was above all a perfectionist, a top-ranking philatelist and appropriately enough a skilled painter of miniatures. Francis Bussell assured me that little Goss as a broker was of outstanding ability. He could present a poor risk dressed up in the attractive raiment which Holy Writ attributes to the Lilies of the Field. I had it from Goss himself that the ragging and gall he often used in his sales pitch especially when aimed at men twice or more his size sometimes resulted in physical reprisals of a kind which only the puckish Goss could suffer with no ill feeling and thereafter recount as amusing experiences.

* * *

During World War I most of us not required for the armed services helped the national effort as best we could on a part-time basis by joining one or other of the many volunteer groups set up to that end. We were *inter alia* Home Guards, Fire Fighters, Ambulance Men and in most of the large towns we were Special (i.e. auxiliary) Constables. In the City of London there was a strict rule that a real, regular policemen had to be at least six feel tall. But no such minimum applied to Specials. And so, and I believe just for the Hell of it, Goss became the smallest City of London Special Constable ever. He regaled me with several racy accounts of his adventures, 'on the beat' and one of them in particular I thought should be immortalised in the LOG. It ran as follows:

ONCE UPON A TIME during the Great War a certain Lloyd's broker became a Special Constable. That he weighed less than seven stone and stood only five feet five in his service boots mattered naught, for he had brain and drive enough to equip ten men twice his size.

Francis Robert Bussell
Portrait by Joan Halifax

Sir Ernest Cooper of Lloyd's, Lord Mayor of London

Walter Farrant (1853–1915), Lloyd's chief 'caller' in the rostrum

S. A. ('Sam') Meacock

John Julius Angerstein (1735–1823)
From a portrait by Sir Thomas Lawrence

Kenneth Frank Stacy

Graham Harding

The 'Room' at Lloyd's

From The Illustrated London News, 11th October, 1890

One night as he trod his beat through the City, his thoughts playing happily upon a neatly baited slip for use on the morrow, his reverie was broken by a bus which drew up at his side. The conductor leaned out and spoke thus: "Orficer, there's a bloke on top wot won't pay 'is fare and won't git orf neether!" So saying he stood back in order that the Orficer might mount the stairs and do his duty. Our hero went aloft with firm resolve. He found there only a single passenger, a huge man some yard and a half across the shoulders, bulging with muscle and far enough gone in drink to have a nasty red gleam in his pig-like eyes. After, as it were, surveying the risk and quoting himself a rate, the Special regained the safety of the kerb. Hand in pocket he turned to the conductor and asked: "How much is his fare?"

Moral: Insure.

THIRTEEN

F. W. MARTEN'S GARDEN PARTY AND TRANSPORT FOR THE BAND

BACK in the days when many City gentlemen lived in such rural areas as Dulwich, Streatham and Tooting Bec they rode to town on horse-back. Their mounts were left for the day in a livery stable kept by one Marten on the south side of London Bridge. During school holidays Marten had help from his young son Freddie whose efficiency greatly impressed the clients and particularly an important Somebody from Lloyd's. The shrewd Freddie may have foreseen that saddlehorses would in a decade or so drop out of use. Or he may have sensed that his wits would have less scope in a loose-box than in a Box at Lloyd's. However that may be it was with high hopes that, his schooling over, he took the helpful hand of that Somebody aforesaid to walk across the Thames to the Royal Exchange. There he rose in the course of time from the lowly post of office boy to that of a Marine underwriter. It is conceded that he was not only 'a' Marine underwriter; he was 'the' Marine underwriter, the finest Lloyd's had ever known. If a broker with a marine risk to place could get F. W. Marten to lead it the market would absorb the rest without a query. In September 1941 'Lloyd's LOG' published my faithful and discreet version of F.R.B.'s Marten yarn and it run thus:

ONCE UPON A TIME in the far-off leisurely days when business tittupped along with easy grace, Lloyd's Chairman was a noble Peer whose duties, compared with those

of today, were light and purely decorative. The Committee, as they have always done, toiled industriously at their current problems, but they were assisted in their labours by The Secretary, a famous and authentic permanent official upon whom long service in the Establishment had bestowed unique authority.

Of azure lineage and military bearing, immaculately garbed and groomed, genial but commanding, he was proud to play the role of Lloyd's Own Particular Personal Representative.

There were giants in the earth in those days and among them was F. W. Marten, surely the greatest marine underwriter who ever initialled a slip. His knowledge was profound, his judgment unerring, and to the ineffable satisfaction of his Names his loss ratio touched the miraculous.

It was his pleasant custom once a year to entertain his Lloyd's friends at a dance in his Hampstead home when hospitality was dispensed so charmingly and so liberally withal that none, without churlishness, could meet it in a frugal spirit.

So delightful and congenial were these gatherings that at the close the company dragged themselves away with reluctance; and this circumstance not unnaturally afforded Mr. Marten a proper and genuine pleasure, and never more than on one famous occasion when the very last to make his tardy adieux was that very essence, epitome and microcosm of Lloyd's of whom we have already made mention, namely, The Secretary himself.

Thanking his host most warmly for a thoroughly enjoyable party and complimenting him upon the excellence of (among other things) the music which had been dispensed, he said he desired the honour of driving to the station in his carriage the bandsmen who had been responsible for this part of the entertainment. Nothing Mr. Marten could say would dissuade him from his hospitable intention.

Now the two outstanding attributes of every really successful underwriter are an immediate and instinctive recognition of snags and the ability to encompass their polite circumvention.

In both those respects Mr. Marten was supremely gifted and it is solely because this particular episode exemplifies the reaction of his great mind to a situation of peculiar delicacy that it finds a place in these chronicles.

The snag which The Secretary in the exuberance of his courtesy had completely overlooked was that his equipage, an old-fashioned but extremely smart brougham, was designed for the accommodation of two passengers only and the transport of the band *en masse* would have demanded something in the nature of a brake.

The circumvention with the co-operation of the musicians was effected thus: The cornet bade good-night to Mr. Marten, touched his hat to The Secretary, stepped into the brougham and quietly stepped out on the far side. He was followed in turn by the fiddle, 'cello, big base drum, basson, flute and euphonium. As they stole silently into the night The Secretary himself, content with all the world, was piped aboard, the coachman whipped up his horse, and with a final valedictory wave of the hand Mr. Marten turned his back upon the scene and upon one more diplomatic triumph.

FOURTEEN

THE FIRE EXTINGUISHER AND WHY IT FAILED

THE next story, while it concerns a certain Lloyd's broker, did not come to me through my Lloyd's work. I heard it by pure chance only a day or two after the happenings related and from one of the very few men who were in the know. At that stage half a century ago my lips were sealed. But the years have rolled away and I now feel free to spill the beans hoping that readers will not think me guilty of what an old law clerk I once knew would have called 'a breach of bad taste'.

ONCE UPON A TIME when the horse-bus had as good as gone, two types of motor-bus took its place; those that ran on petrol and those that went by steam. The steam-bus, quiet and odourless, had one slight fault; now and then it caught fire. As a rule the fire, doused by the hand extinguisher which each bus carried, did small damage. But Lloyd's underwriters, foreseeing whole fleets of buses burned to cinders, allayed their fears by bumping up the relative premiums. The assured's General Manager, an Engineer of genius, tore his hair; he could think of no means by which the current fire losses might be brought nearer zero. Nor was he calmed by the horde of long-haired inventors who plagued him with gadgets guaranteed to make that zero almost a minus quantity. One of these hirsute Edisons when his New Patent Ex-

tinguisher was rejected went over the G.M.'s head to the Board pleading for at least leave to stage a fire, as fierce as you like, and let it be seen how he could put it out in a jiffy. When told of this plea the Lloyd's broker, keen as a fine steel blade, saw a ray of hope. With silvery tongued oratory he urged that the plea be granted. If the device should do its stuff there would be at last some chance of premium reduction. If it should fail no one would be the worse. This oratory won. So the G.M., under his Chairman's orders, built a stout Fifth of November heap in the 'Bus Depot yard ready for the show.

The great day came. In attendance were the broker, the Chairman, the G.M., the inventor and George, a dead-pan Cockney labourer. The heap was lit and blazed merrily.

"Now," called the G.M., "put it out!"

The New Patent Extinguisher went to work. But the flames leaped up as though fed by paraffin. The extinguisher spent itself to the last drop. The fire roared on in triumph!

George was then told, "Bring a bucket of water!" George complying emptied his bucket on the flaming mass. With a 'phutt' the fire was dead.

Sadly, silently, disconsolately, the broker, the Chairman and the inventor stole away.

* * *

Alas! for the Duplicity of Man!

The truth, hidden these fifty years, may now emerge to harm none, all the actors in these events having long since passed away. The pyre, soaked in an evil chemical brew, an incendiary's dream, gave rise to flames which only that brew's chemical antidote could subdue.

And George with his bucket was 'O/C antidote'.

Moral: Grandmas resent instruction in the Art of sucking Eggs.

FIFTEEN

THE LLOYD'S NOTICE-BOARD AND ITS USES BY JOKERS

THE notice-board at Lloyd's carries as a rule announcements of interest only to the Lloyd's community. They are aimed for example at the artistic and athletic circles; support for a tennis tournament is sought, amateur painters and photographers are asked to send in pictures for a forthcoming show and so on. Once in a while, however, an anonymous wag will add to a notice a few bland words which to those in the know, will caustically guy some wretched unnamed victim thought guilty of un-Lloyd's-like behaviour. I recall two examples of such subtle criticism, one cruelly wrong and the other wittily right.

* * *

I have already said that Campbell (my fellow 'W.C.') never forgot the pangs of shyness which wracked him when as a callow youth he had to find out for himself how the Room did its work. Years later, when underwriter in the Matthews Wrightson Box, a youth such as he had been, a mere tyro, came up to him and asked for a Proposal Form. Remembering vividly how savagely he was once slapped down for putting a comparable request to a cantankerous old underwriter instead of going to the old man's junior clerk, he said to the lad, "When you set out for your holidays you don't go to the station-master for your railway ticket, you get it at the ticket window don't you?" "Yes, sir," was the reply. "Well, I'm the station-master here. The ticket window at the other end of this bench is where forms are issued. It's worth bearing that in mind if you don't want to get snubbed." Never had a word of advice been inspired by a kindlier and more unselfish motive. It was given solely to warn a raw beginner against making a humiliating blunder. But the episode was gleefully and inexcusably dished out among a critical young group as an hilarious exhibition of pomposity. And this went the rounds acceptably when Campbell had already incurred unpopularity by his arbitrary and apparently unjustified decision to cut all his renewals of U.S.A. risks by 50%. Events were to prove how right he had been in laying down this rule. But his obstinate refusal to depart from it under strong and authoritative pressure was derided as the most ridiculous eccentricity. And so when a questionnaire pinned on the notice-board called for soccer players to enroll for a match by filling in their names, clubs, and preferred team positions, the inevitable wag obliged by entering:

"Campbell, W. C., Old Station-Masters, Half-linesman." It was undeserved, witty and no doubt it stung.

* * *

The second example of rebuke from the notice-board, well merited and most gently delivered, provided me with a LOG story which appeared in December 1941 and ran thus:

ONCE UPON A TIME early in the morning of 16 September 1913, Augustus George Horn, an Islington artisan on his way to work, retrieved from the London gutter a Bryant & May's matchbox. In so doing he rang the Lutine Bell; for the box contained Mr. Mayer's missing pearl necklace, the finest in the world. There

was accordingly occasion for rejoicing at Lloyd's among those underwriters who insured it for £115,000 and had been mourning its loss for two anxious months.

Exactly how and why these pearls of price came to be so cavalierly jettisoned remains (officially) unexplained. So indeed (officially) does the precise method whereby Messrs. 'Cammi' Grizard, James Lockett, Simon Silverman and Leiser Gutwirth had intercepted this precious string in its registered transit from the Rue de Provence, Paris, to its Hatton Garden destination.

For the purposes of this chronicle, however, we are no more concerned with the elucidation of such mysteries than was the fortunate Augustus George who revelled in his princely reward and let the whys and wherefores go hang. Our interest only arises from the fierce blaze of publicity which beat upon all those who played their parts in the prosecution of the aforesaid malefactors.

"Getting into the papers" strikes the innocent victims of such journalistic attention in various ways; some are annoyed, some pretend to be, some blush, some purr, some giggle but many think it rather a lark and carry the news clippings around to adorn the tale.

It may be assumed that R. D. Muir and Travers Humphreys, prosecuting, and the brave array defending had already been publicised to the point of immunity and met their blurred portraits in the Press without emotion.

The Members of Lloyd's, Mr. Heath and Mr. Mon. Evans and most of their immediate associates in this adventure, although comparative newcomers to the Front Page, faced this photographic ordeal with stoicism. But with the Lloyd's contingent, in constant attendance, if in a comparatively subordinate capacity, was a young broker who, it was thought, looked upon the camera with a friendly eye. He found it, in fact, to be a lark to figure in the illustrated dailies if only as a minnow among the Tritons; and be it said that he was unquestionably photogenic, cultivating a joyful taste in raiment and debonair withal.

When the long Old Bailey trial was well into its stride and public interest was at its height some person or persons unknown exhibited on Lloyd's notice-board a picture cut from the *Daily Splurge*. This picture was of distinct domestic interest. It showed, frozen in the act of leaving the Court buildings, certain distinguished underwriters whose names were duly captioned. Behind them but not thus identified could be seen the handsome face of our young Beau Brummel crowned with a superlative topper whose scintillating highlights inexorably claimed the spectators' attention. A large ink arrow aimed at the very crown of that lustrous head-piece trailed a loop in which was written "The labourer Horn who found the necklace".

SIXTEEN

THE BROKER'S PYJAMAS AND HIS MORNING COAT

THE hunting field sounds an unlikely region in which to pick up a light Lloyd's yarn. But I did it. The Mid-Surrey Drag, of which I was secretary from 1928 to 1931, boasted among its subscribers from time to time during that period at least a score of Lloyd's men. They all rode good horses, they all went well, they all avoided damaging farm land and were consequently very welcome members. The line we ran, never less than ten miles, was always well chosen to give thirty or forty varied and natural jumps. The pack invariably flew hell for leather on a screaming scent (the ball of cotton waste, our 'drag' by which the line was laid, held liquids compounded from our own secret formula; the Zoo bears were most co-operative). The fast and sometimes punishing going made several checks essential to give horses, followers and hounds a breather. The hunting term, 'Coffee-housing' for the talk which enlivens these checks, could not be more apt when those engaged in it were from Lloyd's. At one such check I dropped into conversation with a broker whom I knew well (let us call him Fawkes). He was a tall, handsome, athletic but quiet type. "We've missed you," said I. "I hope your American trip was pleasant and rewarding." "It was," said he, "but for a wretched contretemps." I did not actually say, "Go on" but probably looked it. He continued, "I had just boarded the *Queen Mary* at Southampton when I ran into a friend. He had a youngish girl with him. He introduced us; said she was travelling alone to join her husband in Long Island. Would I very kindly give her a helping hand and so on. I said of course I would and left it at that. It so happened that we were hardly out in the open before we hit heavy seas. They don't worry me; I'm never sick but I always take a lower-deck cabin amidships where the motion is nearly nil and one doesn't get chucked about. I wondered if the girl was all right. I found she had a cabin, one of the worst, on the upper deck well for'ard. Of course, she was as sick as a dog. I sent a message that we must at once swap our quarters. I kept well out of the way. The staff effected the switch. As soon as the poor girl was way down below she must have felt as though she was on dry land. But to make sure I asked the doctor to give her a sedative. I did not see her until the day before we reached New York, fit and well and full of gratitude for my ministering-angel stunt. On arrival [it was a Saturday] her husband was on the dock and pressed me to spend the week-end at their Long Island home. I accepted. Their place was delightful. The husband, twice his wife's age, was most genial, couldn't have been nicer, both of them were. But on the Sunday he was distant, in fact frosty. The wife seemed embarrassed. I hadn't a clue what had gone wrong. Frankly I was glad to get away on the Monday morning with a 'thank you for everything'. But the mystery was solved at my first business call on Wall Street. My pal there grinned and when I asked, "What's the joke?" he gave me a New York Sunday's paper. In it was a bright little account of the switched cabins. The exchange of belongings had been too hasty. When the ship's doctor visited the lady and turned down the coverlet to make with the stethoscope my pyjama suit was revealed.

* * *

It may be thought odd that many years later the LOG would print a story based upon another item of Fawkes' wardrobe.

ONCE UPON A TIME our land being at war, two awkward social problems were created for a certain Member by his son's coming marriage at a very select Regimental Chapel. In the first place there was not nearly enough room to seat all the guests it was wished to invite; Father was at his wit's end to know how, without giving dire offence, still further names could be pruned from an invitation list already cut to the very roots. In the second place he found by survey that his morning coat, once the pride of Savile Row, had by reason of moth, wear and tear and gradual deterioration, become a Constructive Total Loss. And if one has merely a walking-on part at this particular Regimental Chapel a smart morning coat is the least apology one can offer for the lack of a brass hat peaked with golden leaves. At the period of which we write, civilians—even underwriters—might buy clothing only against the surrender of coupons in numbers proportioned to the richness of the apparel sought. Our Member, having a wife and family, it goes without saying was, in terms of coupons, bankrupt.

Now the Member's popularity, which drew friends to him in legions and so gave rise to the first problem, offered an easy solution to the second; he had merely to choose from among those legions a friend of the right

F

shape and generosity and crave from him the loan of the required garment. This was done and with the happy knowledge that his borrowed coat, a triumph of the cutter's art, would pay honour to the ceremony, he sat down once more to the pesky task of docking the nominal roll. This operation seemed already to have reached the irreducible minimum; his eye roved hopelessly down the names until it hit upon that borne by his shapely and generous friend. With a sigh of real regret the Member ran his pen through it saying to himself the while: "How can I possibly invite a chap to a wedding when I know full well he has no morning coat to wear?"

SEVENTEEN

THE BROKER WHO DROPPED BRICKS BUT PROSPERED

GEORGE and I were at the coffee stage. Our talk ambled idly from topic to topic. And a guilty conscience led me to touch upon the *faux pas*, the dropped brick, the clanger.

George shuddered slightly. "Bill," said he, not without a touch of reproach, "you take me back to a painful episode I would fain forget." "Tell me more!" said I. "This," said he, "was long, long ago. Charles and I were on the Continent chasing a big insurance prize. Our Prospect there, a top V.I.P., met us affably and allowed me to hope we might swing the deal. He and his wife were giving a dinner party in our hotel that night for a score of their friends. An invitation was most kindly extended to us. The wife was a beautiful, animated and delightful person. So," continued George, "I was struck by an inspiration. The florist in the hotel foyer had on display superb long-stemmed roses. I slipped Charles a note to have two dozen sent up to our charming hostess at once with my compliments. The lady received them with deep pleasure. I thought even her husband took it well." George eyed me sadly and stopped speaking.

"But George," said I, "this gesture was in the best traditions of gentility! Nobody could possibly equate it with a clanger!"

"Quite," replied he with a bitter laugh, "but I found out too late that the flowers had been charged on the host's dinner account!"

I made sympathetic noises and murmured that maybe the story concealed a moral.

"Bill," said George, "it not only carried a moral, 'Do it yourself and pay cash', it also boasted a happy ending. We landed that prize insurance business and have held it ever since against all comers."

* * *

George I was glad to see was in the mood to talk on. "Bill," said he, "let me tell you of a brick I dropped in Barbados."

"With the aid of a co-director this time?" I asked.

"In a way, yes, but hear me out. Ever been to Barbados?"

"Never," said I.

"Grand spot," said he, "best climate in the West Indies—health resort—sixteenth-century settlement and friendly inhabitants with not a care in the world. So, regarding the rapidly developing popularity of these strategic islands, and one thing and another, you would say we chose well when we set up a link there in our international chain. We liked the place so much and had so many appreciative visitors that way back in 1957 we bought a Regency mansion known as 'Sam Lord's Castle' on high ground by the coast, did it over, put up some small bungalows for extra accommodations and ran the outfit on Country Club lines. For sheer rest and enjoyable relaxation it was unbeatable."

"Sounds enchanting," said I, "but what about the clanger?"

"I am coming to that," said George. "The hospitality we continually received from the island's permanent residents was unending and I laid on a special dinner annually at the Castle to return thanks. All members of the upper crust were represented from His Excellency the Governor down. Some years back my co-director, Ronnie Welch, fell on the rocks after his morning swim and dislocated a shoulder. I went to his bungalow; he was on his feet huddled up in a mauve shot-silk dressing-gown ample enough to hide his surgical strappings. He swore he would be at our swell social dinner that very night. I ordered him under pain of death to attempt no such thing. He pleaded he might at least be allowed to come as he was for pre-dinner cocktails. I slapped this down hard too, promising I would report to him after the show. He seemed to agree. To my horror that evening as I stood at the top of the Castle steps receiving my guests, what should I see, partly hidden from my view by our Club Manager a bit ahead of me, but that mauve-clad figure toiling up towards us! In a loud and angry voice I exclaimed: "Here comes that bloody man and I told him not to be here!" George paused.

"A well merited rebuke," said I.

"But," said George, "when the Manager moved aside the mauve-clad figure turned out to be His Grace the Bishop of Barbados in full ecclesiastical evening dress!"

"Why on Earth," asked George, "do Bishops go around in shot silk?"

I countered this rhetorical question with another. "Why on Earth did Ronnie not wear something more appropriate like Hunting Stewart tartan?"

George snorted.

EIGHTEEN

THE PLANE WHICH CRASHED AMONG THE POULTRY

MANY Lloyd's men, during World War Two, lived in that broad strip of Kent known as 'Bomb Alley', the path by which enemy planes found or tried to find their lethal way to London and, if they were lucky, back again. Each one of those Lloyd's men should he be so disposed could tell a Bomb Alley story out of his own experience. And you may be sure he would not dwell overmuch on blood and havoc. Kind Nature does her best to wipe from our minds the pain of those macabre years. No! The yarn would always invoke a touch of enjoyment, a smile, even a laugh. And this despite its *mis-en-scène*, Kent under constant attack from the sky with Death ever on the prowl for victims. There is but a blurred and meagre margin between tragedy and comedy and for this may we all be thankful. I heard many of these stories in the train when we could not read the evening paper because of the black-out and conversation became an excusable habit. They threw strange side-lights on the armed conflict in which we were all willy-nilly involved. In bulk one could have built a saga from them but so far as I am aware nobody thought of writing them down; like Homer's *Iliad* they passed on and are still occasionally, if in steady lessening volume, passed on by word of mouth. If I were compiling a Bomb Alley saga I might have the temerity to consider two of my own adventures as worthy of inclusion. Firstly that hunting day when I was out with hounds. An R.A.F. formation flying by on another hunting mission, rolled in unison to send the pack a signal which we read loud and clear: "Good show, chaps! Keep it up 'til we are free to join you again! Roger!'. And secondly that Doodle-bug! Its blast sucked out our window glass, lifted our roof tiles and caught my wife in a powdery cloud from our shattered ceilings. A friendly old dame running in to help, not knowing my wife owed her clown-like pallor to pulverised whitewash, threw up her hands and cried: "My dear, you look real bad! Let me get you a nice cuppa?" And thirdly that five mile Sabbath hack across country to take the usual coffee with F.R.B. and his Dinah at their lovely home 'Black Charles'. Our talk was halted by the sound of gunfire. It came, we found, from an aerial dogfight raging too high up for us to tell friend from foe. But the firing ceased; one plane went into a nose dive and a few parachutes floated earthwards. The diving plane crashed a hundred yards from where we stood, its swastika still visible in the wreckage. Riding home I had to pass it. My horse shied at a tarpaulin which hid what was left of the pilot. I jogged along wondering whether or not the parachutists had landed safely. A bridle path led me through a dense coppice. There I overtook a quiet little man in tweedy walking attire. He carried an ash plant in one hand and a small paper bag in the other.

"Fine day," said I in salutation.

"It is indeed, sir," said he.

"Seen any parachutists around?" I asked.

"Yes, sir," said he. "A little while ago a German airman gave himself up to me. He spoke no English but I pocketed his pistol and made him understand by pulling his arm that he must come with me. Fortunately we soon met a squad of soldiers searching the area so I was quit of him!"

"Nice work," said I. "Enjoy your lunch!"

No doubt he did, maybe on a mossy bank where the wild thyme grew and whence one could see Kent spread out in rural beauty, calm after that man-made storm.

As for Bomb Alley tales available from the general pool,

pride of place, in my judgment, must go to the following which has at least three compelling characteristics; it is bizarre, it is unbelievable and it is true. Since it concerns a distinguished Lloyd's underwriter I fall for the temptation to present it in Lloyd's LOG uniform.

ONCE UPON A TIME there lived an underwriter (let us call him Patrick O'Brien) whose extensive Kentish acres well justified his name in Burke's *Landed Gentry*. That his mansion was plumb in the line along which enemy aircraft jettisoned bombs they had been prevented from dropping on London was a nuisance from several points of view; deep craters were made in harmless pastures, cattle were startled and, one assumes even to the regret of the Nazis, foxes were driven away from several of the West Kent Hunt's best coverts. Nights were rendered baleful and grief-ridden by these continual visitations.

While destruction from the sky levelled alike Princes' palaces and poor men's cottages, it also levelled the customary barriers of class. No sooner did disaster strike than the whole neighbourhood rushed to lend a helping hand. And so when Mr. O'Brien, in the small hours, heard the scream and deafening crash of a falling plane he at once ran out to find the wreck and help in any way he might. He did not have far to run; a British plane, a freighter, happily crewless had smashed itself to smithereens upon a neighbouring farmer's fowl houses. A few surviving chickens, philosophically making the best of things, were greedily pecking away under the wreckage. Mr. O'Brien was deeply moved. In the first place by relief that there was so little material damage and no personal injury. In the second by wide-eyed astonishment in recognising the freighter as one part of whose cargo was insured with his own Syndicate at Lloyd's. He even remembered the nature of that part. "Let me," said he to the farmer, "buy these homeless birds for cash and take them off your hands here and now." The transaction was carried through accordingly. It was in fact a Syndicate transaction and the thinking behind it was this; underwriters paying the inevitable total loss on the insured goods would, in law, stand possessed of any salvage they might be able to recover and the sooner the salvage operations began the better. 'Operations' is the governing word. And when those homeless birds were opened they surrendered not only their lives but also the insured cargo which they had so greedily gobbled up—to wit glittering diamonds.

Moral: The wise man values his crops.

NINETEEN

A TRUE GHOST STORY

SIR HUMPHRY DAVY, having no use for ghosts, said, "If you think you see one," he advised, "poke a finger in your eye. If you still see only one while seeing two of everything else the ghost is merely imaginary." But despite such scientific cynicism the craving to believe in worldly visitations by the Departed is insatiable and more so than ever in wartime when we all walk in the very Valley of the Shadow. Your true fanatic is impervious to facts; he does not let them shake his faith. Never was an Old Contemptible, surviving the 1914 blood-soaked Mons retreat, heard to claim that he and his comrades were aided by visible Spirits from the Beyond. Arthur Machen, a journalist, describing this historic battle, adopted poetic prose and said the army's escape was as miraculous as if a Heavenly Host of Angels, white-clad and wielding flaming swords, had barred the enemy's advance. This innocent journalistic fancy has become a phrase and a fable. The 'Angels of Mons' are now accepted as an actual phenomenon which lifted our soldiers' hearts in a dread critical moment. The Law of Supply and Demand is inescapable. Those yearning for a message from a loved one on the Other Side are easy meat for Mr. Sludge, the medium, who in dim-lit seances with soft music and cheesecloth Spirits produces the 'Communication'. Given a chance to investigate these manifestations the trickery emerges as too childishly simple, one would think, to deceive any reasonably intelligent person; but it does. A prime example on which I had the happiness to intrude was 'Borley Rectory, the Most Haunted House in England', the subject of two books and much speculation.[1] After mature, open-minded consideration I found myself unable to give credit to the resident spectres for burning down that dilapidated architectural monstrosity. And neither the Headless Man nor the Hooded Monk, I felt sure, had played any part in procuring the grossly inflated Fire Policy. In fact the relatively few cases in which it was my professional duty to examine supernatural goings-on all fell into the same disappointing pattern. Ghosts could not stand me. So soon as I was spotted they not only faded away, they reassumed, as the phrase goes, 'the trappings of mortality'. The poltergeist whom I 'laid' for on Oxbridge College turned into a lass who had only just put her hair up. The unseen ghost who wished poor old A to make a Will in favour of B and wrote faint spirit demands to that effect on B's mirrors (with toilet soap) cast himself for the role of a very earthy individual weak on spelling and wearing rough tweed reach-me-downs. Strive as I might, facts to prove that ghosts existed or that they didn't eluded me. Patently non-psychic but undismayed by past experience, still hoping for something really baffling in the occult line to turn up it may be imagined with what joy I met post war a 100% non-psychic lady from Lloyd's with a tale to tell right up my street.

And here it is:

Once Upon A Time—perhaps in the 1920s—certain Lloyd's brokers, needing office accommodation, seized the opportunity of buying the freehold of an unique City property. Built shortly after the Great Fire of 1666 it fell no doubt into the third classification of standardised houses permitted by the City Fathers

[1] See my *Far from Humdrum* Chap. 23 and *The Haunting of Borley Rectory* by Dingwall, Goldney and Hall (Gerald Duckworth) 1956.

'of the least sort' and stood three floors high but cottage-like in what was then its modest flower garden.

Two and a half centuries had given it jostling and formidable neighbours of steel and concrete, the garden had become a paved court, and its path had grown into the almost indestructible possession of the commonalty—a public right of way.

Maybe you have brushed it with your left elbow on your way to Simpsons' Cheese Guessing, or more probably with the other on your way back.

Its former owner, a worthy old lawyer, had been snatched away from this world so tragically and suddenly that the newcomers found it difficult to believe he would never more be back to pursue his calling; legal documents bestrewed the desks, pens and inks stood ready to write 'without prejudice' and postage stamps curled up in the petty-cash box.

There was in fact so firm a background of familiar things, so compelling a notion of a personal presence, that when, in the evening hush, Someone, who was not there in the flesh, was heard trotting up and down the stairs or moving in an empty room, no surprise was occasioned—it all seemed perfectly normal and above everything, friendly.

And then on 29th December 1940, enemy bombs with malevolent fury, searched out this quiet City backwater; some of the proud neighbouring office blocks crumbled into elemental dust, but our dignified little establishment came through unscathed.

Next day an elderly lady with the dress and mien of a bygone generation called there and introduced herself as the widow of the former occupant; her purpose was not apparently to congratulate the Lloyd's brokers upon their providential escape but to assure them, lest they should have any apprehensions in the matter, that no harm would come to her late husband's premises "whatever might happen".

Her manner was not that of one merely seeking to inspire faith: she was stating a scientific fact. With an encouraging nod of her bonnet she departed and has been seen no more.

On 10th May 1941, all the adjacent properties which had survived the earlier attack were burned and blasted to destruction, while that small and aged habitation, still intact, heroic and indomitable, stood four-square to the horrid sea of desolation fulfilling the gentle widow's prophecy.

But go and look for yourself and in future when Peter Pan asks if you believe in fairies you may be inclined to clap.

TWENTY

FRANK STACY AND HIS GOOD WORKS IN SEVENOAKS

SEVENOAKS at night in wartime was a dreary place for soldiers on short leave, at a loose end, far from home and friends. The 'pubs' it is true, if open, gave a spot of comfort, some weak beer and even a game of darts. Frank Stacy of Lloyd's felt the need to do a bit better than this and being Frank Stacy he did it. He took a few rooms over a shop in the High Street. One of them was large; it would hold a score of men at a pinch. Tea, coffee and cocoa when available could be brewed in the ancient kitchen. There were newspapers and magazines, there were writing facilities, there was a piano on which Frank would play whatever he might be asked to play all the way from a Bach Fugue down to (or up to?) 'On Ilkla Moor Bart 'At'. Above all there was light, warmth and a free and easy atmosphere in which his visitors could stretch out their legs and just relax. Frank soon found that hardly any of the men using this port o' call had the least idea how a City gent such as he made a living. In a chat with a number of them round the fire he described in simple terms how insurance is run and why and explained his own role in it. Keen questioning followed—(Audience Participation!) and so much interest was shown in what to the listeners was a New World that he asked: "Would you like to receive some other City type if I could get one along?" The answer was a unanimous "Yes!". Thus began what were to be known as 'Fireside Chats'.

The first victim was I think a Big Noise, a Jobber, from

the Stock Exchange. Somewhere along the line Frank dragged in a Bank Chairman, a top-ranking Railway Executive, a Land Surveyor, a Swell from a City Livery Company and a Produce Broker, all of them fellow travellers on the Sevenoaks–London train. Frank was sure that these informal gatherings and the obvious pleasure which the respective Chatterers took in getting together with the Lads on a basis of equality did a great deal towards bridging the social class gap which is so wide in peacetime and so narrow under the impact of war when we all face the same perils whoever we may be.

He kept me in touch; the chats were going well. But I smelt a rat when he began telling me of his difficulties in finding City Gents from new fields ready and willing to perform. He eyed me much as a cannibal chief might when speculating whether or not a captive was fit for the stew pot. In the end of course my turn came. I chose for my theme 'Crime as a Career'. I based this chat on the supposition that a proportion of those then crowding round me might decide, when peace broke out, that rather than resume a life of uninspiring honest toil they would follow one in a chosen sphere of crime as being the more attractive cash-wise and the less exhausting. For those supposedly making this latter choice I gave tips of a practical nature on what they must do and above all what they must not do if they were to merit any reasonable success in their unlawful enterprises.

First I told them they must work alone and let no other crook in on what was afoot since a thief is notoriously without honour and never to be trusted. This means I said that if theft is the chosen ploy only unidentifiable items must be stolen (ideally metal money) otherwise a 'fence' is your only market and of all soulless rapacious sharks who batten on men trying to make a dishonest living your 'fence' pollutes the bottom-most dregs. Given courage, a cool head, common sense and a decent slice of luck and accepting a spell in jail now and then as a normal occupational hazard, your malefactor, I promised, might live for brief periods at liberty if not with an easy mind at least with a full belly. Passing from the general to the particular I related the story of Flannel Foot, a burglar who stuck so closely to the rules I had outlined that he went undetected for twelve years. He broke into the modest homes of working-class folk and always on paydays. He knew that after the usual cheery night at the 'local' the wage earner and his spouse would be abed and very fast asleep indeed. The Law deals severely with persons caught 'carrying housebreaking implements by night'. Neither Flannel Foot nor the tool bag on his push-bike carried anything of such a guilty nature. But the bag did hold an innocent little bradawl which in his highly-trained hand would open any suburban kitchen window in a matter of seconds. He invariably entered by the kitchen because of its situation (at the rear of the house and out of sight of passers-by) and because, justifying his sobriquet, he could take from the sink the flannels which would be wrapped round his feet to deaden his footsteps and to eliminate the risk of leaving telltale shoe marks on the lino. Encouraged by the stertorous breathing of the sleeping couple he would go softly into the bedroom, collect the cash from the side table or from the trousers (either hung on a bedpost or chair or slung in a heap on the floor) and get back to his bike and dissolve into the flood of other cyclists pedalling to their early morning shifts. But in the end the inevitable oversight gave him away. One cannot think of everything. Wifeless, he lived in a small North London house alone with his only child, a wee girl. Flannel Foot would tuck her up in bed to sleep with a 'Good night' kiss before setting forth on his usual forays. What he over-looking was the possibility that the little girl, now a prattling toddler, might have inherited papa's adventurous spirit and nocturnal habits. Sure enough the time arrived when a friendly copper found her, dressed and self-confident, taking a walk abroad around 11 p.m. and quite willing to join him on his beat.

At the Police Station over a cup of cocoa she told the nice officer where she lived and how her daddy went out at nights and when he came back how he poured lots and lots of lovely silver pennies into her bed for her to play with. Daddy when reclaiming his missing daughter was greatly disturbed by her childish prank. He was even more greatly disturbed when 'tecs who had been stealthily on his heels for weeks caught him as he emerged from his umpteenth kitchen window. No one must, I said, take Flannel Foot's amazing record as a precedent or think me so stupid as to brag that by sticking to the Crocker Rules your cracksman or any other criminal could hope to keep clear of clink for more than six months, probably less. I gave a further warning to any optimist who thought he might beat my gloomy forecast and it was this: of all the snags which bestrew the crook's path on his way to jail personal habits or skills perhaps present the deadliest danger. Examples? Take the 'wanted' waiter who dining on the Blue Train helps himself to a potato by the expert use of a spoon and fork in one hand. Or the hasty fellow who quarrels too violently with a girl and is obliged to cord her body in sacking for convenient disposal. He uses knots which only a seaman could make. Or the unknown who writes threatening letters always five words to a line (a telegraphist) and so on in thousands of recorded cases and in thousands more to come. I advised strongly against insurance swindles as too full of pitfalls to be worth the gamble and too difficult to engineer anyway. My audience seemed to enjoy instances of frauds which had failed so I told them about the man who would plant a sliver of suet on the sole of his shoe and then fall heavily in front of a butcher's shop. Clasping his wrist in feigned agony he would be taken to a nearby surgery. There the doctor would see the reddened skin and feel the displaced bone. A suitable splint would be supplied and the 'injured' man would as soon as possible accept a reasonable sum in settlement of damages. The displacement, in fact an irregular bony union, was a relic of a genuine accident ten years before. The inflammation was produced by vigorous rubbing with a piece of wood. The scene was staged again repeatedly within a month at several butchers' shops miles apart all the way from Land's End to John o' Groats. What this ingenious rascal did not know was that his intended victims, while trading hundreds of miles from one another were all insured through their Trade Association under the same general Policy. So all his claims fell to be handled by one and the same adjuster and proved to be worth no more than free lodgings and keep by courtesy of H.M. Government. Fire claims I dismissed as too dangerous even for the most highly experienced arsonists and I referred my listeners to newspaper reports for confirmation of that view.

Having mentioned if only briefly every type of crime in which the members of my audience as amateurs could be expected to engage I had the comfortable sensation, not I hope too conceitedly, that with one exception they were with me to a man. That one exception was a mature, well-built soldier in his mid-twenties sitting slap in front of me. From the very start of the meeting, while not inattentive he had looked sour, almost derisive, and apparently held both me and my inconsequential observations in something like contempt. This was disconcerting and puzzling and I wondered if at any time unknown to me he and my firm had crossed swords. When I asked him to give me his usual signature on my writing pad so that I might demonstrate a useful method of forgery he complied at once. To turn the signature upside down and copy it was a simple exercise in freehand drawing, an old parlour trick which I had performed many times. In this instance I hope I may be excused for saying the result was excellent. I explained that a forger copying a signature right way up would unconsciously tend to use his own style of making individual letters whereas in drawing the upsidedown version he would merely be copying a meaningless pattern with no recognisable letters to lead him astray. Was I right in thinking that when my derisive friend inspected the forgery of his own signature he looked up at me with mild surprise, almost respect as though thinking 'This bloke is not as boneheaded as I thought he was!' But why the chip on his shoulder? I was sure he had never fallen foul of me in the past. His name, a most unusual one, would have stamped itself on my memory.

Next morning, the affair still rankling in my mind, I asked a detective friend was anything 'known' about this sour puss? The reply came through: "We have a Provincial warrant for his arrest on a charge of burglary. Where is he?" Speaking the literal truth I said I did not know. But could one have a finer specimen of the crook's 'oversight' and 'lack of thought'. The most ordinary caution should have warned this dolt that with my quite apparent interest in criminality I was not the sort of person to be trusted. Yet he blindly gave me his real name when he could just as easily have given me a false one. Only my kind heart and the sympathy I felt for any soldier on his way to the front (and maybe a sneaking thought that Frank would dislike the idea of one of his guests being pinched through me) saved him from arrest and prosecution.

TWENTY-ONE

HIS ROLE IN LLOYD'S ADOPTION OF H.M.S. *IMPLACABLE*

KENNETH FRANK STACY, slim, fair and neat, a bachelor, lived with his widower father in a cosy house tucked out of sight at the old end of Sevenoaks. Its trim garden backed on to the Tudor park of Knole; the fourteenth-century Sevenoaks Grammar School was but a stone's-throw away. He and I as near neighbours often taking the City train and the occasional cup of coffee together and swapping Lloyd's gossip were destined to develop a warm friendship. After six years in the Room, Frank (I knew nothing about the 'Kenneth') was made an Underwriting Member and ultimately became underwriter for the powerful Gardner Mountain and D'Ambrumenil Marine Syndicates. His devotion to Lloyd's was profound. He regarded his success there as due solely to unmerited luck and his kind heart moved him to promote happiness whenever he could among folk he felt were more deserving of it than he had been. His promotional activities took many forms and I pleasurably recall another example of them.

* * *

In 1942 Frank gave deep thought to the subject of adoption. He was not out to adopt a baby but a battleship. His choice was the Fleet aircraft carrier H.M.S. *Implacable* of 20,000 tons displacement then under construction. His idea he sold to the Committee with the greatest of ease and the ship was formally adopted by Lloyd's in March 1942. She was to carry a complement of some 2,000 souls and Frank believed that, apart from the proud silk ensign already given by Lloyd's, 'Articles, substantial, useful, Officers, N.C.O.s and other ranks for the use of' might be appreciated. He sent a slip outlining this notion round the Room Box by Box inviting small subscriptions in support of it. "The result," Frank told me, "was a near Disaster! So much money poured in that I feared we should never be able to spend it all!" But with imagination and suggestions from 'Dick' Knight, the ship's Chaplain, it was all satisfactorily consumed. Books and a complete library of gramophone discs, helped, silver ashtrays and the like helped a bit more and I faintly remember something about brass for the band, a tiger-skin for the big drum major and gauntlet gloves for whom or for what purpose I have long since forgotten. The Royal Navy was grateful and when the Royal Navy is grateful it likes to do something about it. In this instance the 'something' emerged as a proposition that a delegation of Lloyd's members, as many as could be persuaded to do so, should travel up to Rosyth to see the ship and enjoy a spot of hospitality. But the war, annoying and inconvenient in so many ways, made it difficult to put this plan into effect. On the one hand *Implacable*, busy keeping watch over the *Tirpitz* in Tromsö Fjord and in making a nuisance of herself generally among enemy shipping, could not for the moment fix a date for the projected Rosyth 'At Home'. And on the other hand Lloyd's Committee was coping practically night and day with the incredibly difficult war insurance problems thrown up for them and the Government paled at the thought of releasing members at any time for a joyride to Scotland and back. Nevertheless at long last, in March 1945, *Implacable* stopped for a breather, a tired team of five Representative Lloyd's men[1] dropped work for a bit and the party was

[1] T. L. Forbes (Chairman of Price, Forbes & Co.) in command, Matthew Drysdale, 'Toby' Green, George Mac G. Harper (alias 'Mac' Harper) and Kenneth Frank Stacy (Hon. Sec.).

on. "And what a party!" said Frank. "If we looked just a drab City bunch when faced by the slick R.N. spit and polish, the smart uniforms and the snap of Navy discipline, no one let us dwell on it. The Ship was ours! We were met with heart-warming smiles from the officers who wined—repeat wined—and dined us and from the unsleeping Jeeves-like Marines who valeted us round the clock. The Wardroom banquet was superb and in the light of wartime rationing, miraculous. The prevailing note was one of levity. It is true that in a delightful speech of welcome Captain Hughes-Hallet[1] asked us to share his controversial view that control of the Air over the Navy should be a job for the Navy and not for the Royal Air Force. Tom Forbes replied with his well-known charm and tact and left everyone happier than ever. I recall vaguely that after dinner there was heightened hilarity and song. I hope I proved my own sobriety by taking to the piano in my shirt sleeves and banging away loud if not clear. Some of our hosts proved theirs—or did they?—by doing hair-raising 'dags'. One daredevil Pilot Officer crawled along a steel deck-beam over a hangar and hung from it by his feet head down with a "Look, Ma! No hands!" I was horrified! Regaining safety he hinted that maybe the guests could offer a 'dag' of some sort. One of our number who shall be nameless[2] thereupon fell into a Buddhistic state of Self Contemplation. Awakening from it he asked solemnly: "Can the Mess find me a pint tankard of ale?" The Mess could and did. (*Implacable* had everything.) Our member, our Champion indeed, then stood on his head and holding that antipodal position quite steadily drank the ale to the very last drop. I felt a surge of pride. Lloyd's had once again risen to a challenge and beaten it!"

[1] Later Vice-Admiral Sir Cecil Charles Hughes-Hallett, K.C.B. [now decd.].

[2] It was in fact 'Mac' Harper who said he learned the trick as a Gunner in World War I and won much free beer thereby.

TWENTY-TWO

THE ICE SHIP

HERBERT SPENCER in his *Essays on Education* asked 'Why do we smile when a child puts on a man's hat?' Why do we split our sides when we see a man or even an old lady tread on a banana skin and go head over heels? What is there so funny in the time-worn custard pie technique? Spencer, that fascinating philosopher, has it worked out physiologically all the way from the coy smirk to the helpless roll in the aisle. Mostly the answer is said to be that when we see someone either put into a ridiculous situation or like a skilful clown pretends to be, we feel relatively superior and are thereby amused. Grock struggling to push his grand piano closer to his music stool or Charlie Chaplin on the verge of starvation in Alaska delicately eating his boiled boots; here the comedy was tinged with pathos, but comedy triumphed. For Lloyd's men the ridiculous situations were nearly always deliberately created. Here however is the story of an exception.

ONCE UPON A TIME a Lloyd's broker, young, acute, resourceful and oh! so energetic, was instructed to effect re-insurances in respect of Total Loss Only and Fire upon a fleet of liners. The order was gigantic; the broker's cup of joy would have been full to the brim but for the lamentable fact that an order of this kind seemed almost incapable of execution. A steady rise in values on the one hand and a spate of calamities on the other had created a market so nervous that Fire Man-

agers, at the merest hint of such business, keened like banshees and ran for home.

Nevertheless and to the wonder of everybody, the Young Broker, with a magician's touch, placed his order to the very last farthing. It was a notable triumph which the Young Broker decided he could only fittingly celebrate by entertaining the Fire Managers who had written the Risk and so made that triumph possible. Those good gentlemen, still under the spell, graciously accepted his invitation. One of London's most famous restaurants was selected. The choice of fish, flesh, fowl and vintage was made in an almost religious conference with the *maître d'hôtel*. The sweet, it was agreed, should be left to the inspiration of the chef, an artist whose culinary works would not have disgraced the Royal Academy's Summer Exhibition.

One can picture the meal; a slightly frigid start, the guests perhaps as surprised to find themselves at the Young Broker's table as they had been to find themselves on his slip, a gradual mellowing under the influence of good food, good wine and good fellowship, spirits ultimately rising to the unspoken thought, "God's in His heaven, all's right with the world" and then—a pause for the great moment, the advent of the sweet. What will it be? Something novel and appropriate if the chef's reputation in such matters is really merited.

The *maître d'hôtel* enters smiling and majestic, bearing

an enormous dish aloft. He waits, confidently, for the applause which always greets this spectacle. Instead he is met by a sudden and ominous hush, by eyes all fixed in horror on his burden, by faces manifesting grief, gloom, woe and despair.

For the chef's *chef-d'œuvre* is a luxury liner, a miracle of the confectioner's art, floating in an ocean of liqueur. But alas! the sea is a sea of flame and the proud vessel is ablaze from stem to stern.

TWENTY-THREE

'SAM' MEACOCK AND HIS STORY OF THE LOST YACHT

SAM MEACOCK came to Lloyd's in 1873. He died seventy-seven years later at nearly ninety-four. Over three-quarters of a century in the Room! What a tale he could have told had he been so minded! What changes he had seen, from sail to steam, from the horse and buggy to the Ford, from the reign of tall ships to that of aviation. With his sturdy build and weathered face, his quiet voice and kindly, tolerant ways, he had more the cut of the shires about him than that of the City in which he made so great a success.

Though far from taciturn he rarely spoke of the old days. Even when he did, under my urging, there was often a touch of sly mockery in what he said.

In the Captains' Room after lunch when the chance offered I would join him at his table to take a coffee while he took, not a glass of port, but a tankard of ale. In this it was his habit to stir a small crust of bread impaled on a fork. (I have never seen this ancient rite of 'the Toast' performed by anyone else.) With a slow swirl of the fork and a puff at his cigar, Mr. Meacock (he was always 'Mister' to me, thirty years his junior) would respond to my pumping with an amused smile on his face.

"Was your father a Londoner, Mr. Meacock?"

"No, he was a farmer."

"You were raised in the country then?"

"Yes: as a child I used to perch on our farm gate to watch the Bath Mail Coach drive through the village."

"Where was the farm?"

"Middlesex."

"What was the name of the village?"

"Hammersmith."

"Hammersmith!"

"Yes, in 1869 you could walk across the fields all the way from there to Ealing without seeing so much as a barn. After that you came to a big house." Pause for a sip of ale and solemn reflection, and then as though imparting information of the deepest gravity, "It belonged to the tight-rope walker Blondin."

Mr. Meacock never seemed to be old, yet few in the Room were his seniors and from this he drew a bit of wry satisfaction.

John, his son, an undergraduate at Cambridge, rode with the Mid Surrey Drag when I was secretary. John had a hunting companion, a likeable and wealthy young man, who for present purposes shall be called "Porgey". I knew that Porgey, probably at the behest of John, was offered the valuable privilege of joining the Meacock's Syndicate. But nothing came of it and I did not learn why until maybe three decades later. The subject cropped up when Mr. Meacock and I were discussing, of all odd subjects, solicitors.

"Porgey would have made a fortune had he joined my Names in 1915," said he, "but his solicitor urged him not to because of my advanced years—I was sixty."

"What on earth was the solicitor's name?" I asked.

"I don't remember," said Sam, and slowly dunking his toast and then looking me sadly in the eye he added, "he died a long, long time ago."

I can date one of our chats; it must have been in 1945. The topic, raised as usual by me, was The Past as known to Mr. Meacock. He suddenly broke off and paused.

Lowering his voice he asked, "You have heard that my sister died?"

I was shocked, said I had not been told about it, and how

sorry I felt for him. It then entered my mind that since he was in his late eighties his sister would have been a very old lady. I asked, "When did she die?"

He stirred his ale reflectively and replied, "Let me see. Father was born in 1799. He first married at eighteen and the girl was born—Good Lord she has been dead a hundred and twenty-five years. How Time does fly!"

This leg-pull so typical of his special brand of humour was easy to take. It weighed little against the many fascinating stories I dug out of him; of his start as office boy in one Lloyd's firm and his shift to another where he became confidential clerk and book-keeper to a Mr. Stearns, an underwriter with a small Marine Syndicate.

"My boss," he told me, "never liked his seat in the Room to be left unoccupied so I had to go and sit in it when he went to lunch. I got the hang of the job and soon found myself acting as deputy during Mr. Stearn's holidays. The passing years were kind to me. They have floated me up from deputy to principal with Names of my own. Lots of luck and lots of fun!"

He read 'Lloyd's Log' regularly. When I confided to him that I was the anonymous writer of the *Once Upon A Time* series and pleaded for a publishable yarn, he told me one which, with such delicacy as I could command, I dressed up as follows:

ONCE UPON A TIME said the Oldest Active Underwriter: "When the Register, save for one page of steamers, was devoted entirely to sailing ships, the Comic Muse with bewildering perversity hand in hand with tragedy, visited the very Box in which I worked."

He hesitated: "But you may think this rather a vulgar story. Perhaps I had better not go on."

"Sir," we replied firmly, "historians cannot afford to

be squeamish. We are historians. Pray proceed."

"Well," said the O.A.U., "you must know that my guv'nor was the recognised market for the insurance of those small yachts which, in the holiday seasons of that epoch, took parties of 'swells' cruising around our shores and across Channel to the suspect pleasures of Ostend and Boulogne.

"One such craft, thoroughly seaworthy, stoutly built, freshly painted with scarlet bottom and cream upper works, dragged her anchor in the night and entirely vanished from the sight of her amateur crew who were larking ashore. She sounded like a total loss (by no means the first of the kind). However, following the usual routine, we wired her name, *The Bride,* to all appropriate Lloyd's Agents and warned them to be on the watch for her. Perchance she might, by good fortune, drift to safety. Sure enough and against all probabilities she did turn up in Belfast Harbour. Lloyd's Agent there could hardly believe his eyes. Wishing to confirm that this vessel of a not uncommon name, was in fact the craft concerned, he telegraphed my guv'nor as the leading underwriter, for further information." The O.A.U. shook his head sorrowfully. "I can see that telegram now," he murmured.

"Has *The Bride* got. . . ."

"Don't tell us," we interrupted. "The Agent doubtless sought to identify the vessel by reference to the red paint on her; that is, from keel to water line?"

"Exactly," answered the O.A.U. "Of course, the Agent, in all innocence, employed the technical and time-honoured word for that special part of the hull."

"But was that in any sense unfortunate?" we asked. "You spoke of tragedy?"

"It was very unfortunate indeed," replied the O.A.U. "You see, my guv'nor, a confirmed bachelor, had in late middle age decided to take a wife. He was sensitive about it; he feared his friends in the Room might pull his leg. The Agent's telegram greeted him on his return from the honeymoon."

The O.A.U. puffed reflectively at his after-lunch cigar. "To his dying day," he said, "my guv'nor thought someone had put the Agent up to it."

TWENTY-FOUR

ABOUT TIN CANS AND CHINESE CRACKERS

THE out-and-out practical joke was rare at Lloyd's. I can recall very few. One was an unplanned jape, hatched from the Rule that in the New Lloyd's, to which members moved on leaving the Royal Exchange, there should be No Smoking. Men who lined up to show risks at underwriters' Boxes often had to wait a long time for their turn to come. Meanwhile, deprived of the soothing gasper their sufferings were deplorable. In sheer pity certain underwriters provided boiled sweets for them to suck. By pure chance one day an empty sweet tin fell to the floor and rolled down the marble steps which led to the telephone kiosks. In so doing, it revealed that the accidental acoustical properties of those steps and marble-lined walls fell little short of those boasted by Sir Christopher Wren's Whispering Gallery at St. Paul's. This phenomenon promised a lark too good to be wasted. Surreptitiously grey-haired members competed with teenagers to start cans bumping along on their clamorous way to beat the band.

For some this echoing clatter struck a cheery note with a ring of boyish mischief about it; for others, the majority, it was an infernal nuisance, and Lloyd's Committee sat to find a cure. One of the members (call him Seaman) said in effect, "My Box being closest to the scene of this trouble, I suppose I get more of the din than anyone else and I hope this Committee will ask that if the provision of bull's eyes and such is to continue, metal containers shall give way to paper bags." It was an ingenious solution. But

Seaman was nothing if not ingenious and imaginative. He had indeed demonstrated these qualities by inventing and thereafter secretly performing the Rolling Can malarky.

* * *

The F.R.B. story which I class with this must be dated well before World War I when hearts were young and gay. It made its bow in the LOG for January 1942 and ran thus:

Once Upon A Time if the legend be accepted, a benign Chinaman idly mixing the saltpetre from his cooking pot with the charcoal from his fire, accidentally produced the forefather of gunpowder. To his delight he found that this novel concoction could be persuaded to ignite with an amusing report. It was but a step from this to the Chinese Cracker which, under Divine inspiration, he dedicated to the Worship of his Honourable Ancestors and the general discomfiture of Devils. With what sorrow would this gentle Celestial have learned that the passage of a few thousand years would see his pious firework bring shameful calamity upon a Member of Lloyd's.

The sad story is soon told. The Member in question, in whose veins ran the mingled blood of England, Ireland and France, was, as might be anticipated from such corpuscular equipment, of a mercurial temperament, swinging from one emotion to another with kaleidoscopic facility. When a cracker was tossed spluttering beneath his seat he made frantic efforts to foot it out clear of his Box, where it might be smothered before the first of its many potential detonations could insult the ear of the Room. More haste begot less speed; but finally the fuming Member, surprised and relieved that the impending bang had been so long delayed managed to plant his heel on the sizzling menace. The Joker (we suppress his name for the family's sake) stood brazenly by, chuckling with joy. He explained that his particular brand of cracker was a mere dummy; it was designed to create alarm and apprehension but no noise above a whisper. The Member's fury gave way immediately to bubbling merriment. This, thought he, was a creamy prank worthy of emulation. He extracted from the Joker a promise to bring him another dummy on the morrow and in consultation with that expert chose the next victim, a particularly inoffensive and retiring Underwriter of advanced years who transacted his business at a Box nearby.

Next day the Member duly lit and threw his dummy. He had the mirthful satisfaction of seeing in his respectable victim's startled reactions all those which he himself had so recently exhibited in similar circumstances.

The Joker vanished.

And then the "dummy" deafened the Room with the first of its thirty explosions.

It had to run its course; a leaping mob, however intent on fire extinction is no match for a leaping firework whose path is unpredictable.

The Member, penitent and metaphorically white-sheeted, made his difficult apologies to an outraged Committee. Among other even less palatable things they said, in effect, what Good Queen Victoria had said a few years before: "We are not amused."

TWENTY-FIVE

THE CHURCHWARDEN UNDERWRITER AND THE DOUBTFUL OFFERINGS

THE Captains' Room in the Royal Exchange was a cosy place in which to take the morning coffee and the midday meal. It wore an old-time air of solidarity as if in direct descent from Edward Lloyd's establishment. The heavy dining-tables, benches and partitions dated from the eighteenth century. The patrons, save now and then for a rare visitor, were in the eighteenth-century sense of the term 'Regulars'. Everyone knew everybody else, at least by sight, and each had by courtesy a seat sacred to himself alone. The daily encounters in such a genial atmosphere naturally encouraged occasional leg-pulls and decorous pleasantries. Presiding over all was the smiling 'Fred', catering manager, cashier and long-standing familiar of the *habitués*. He enjoyed with them the sort of quasi-feudal relationship which was extended to several of the old hands on Lloyd's staff, Walter Farrant, the famous caller, being the supreme example. The high regard in which 'Fred' was held even, at times, implicated him personally in some of the Captains' Room larks. One of these I recorded in the LOG for April 1942 and it ran as follows:

ONCE UPON A TIME there lived a Churchwarden whose habit it was, in the conduct of his virtuous office, to adhere to those admirable principles which governed his more worldly activities as an Underwriting Member of Lloyd's. From the Sabbath offertory, for instance, he

scrupulously extracted all impertinent though lamentably prevalent items such as French *sous*, leaden florins, off-colour shillings and whatnot, took these down as a total loss, replaced them with good currency and stood subrogated to the salvage.

Trouser buttons and similar deliberately jettisoned tokens thereafter presented no difficulty. For them he established a fixed exchange in terms of sterling: bone buttons in mint condition being "pegged" at threepence a dozen. The disposal of his main haul, the foreign and otherwise doubtful coinage, called for rather more diplomacy.

On Mondays, after lunch, in the old Captains' Room, he spread his drab collection on the table cloth and invited his colleagues to bid for any specimen whose claim to legitimacy was not manifestly incredible. This plan never failed. But invariably, of all the bids, the most spirited came from a popular broker who loved two things with equal fervour: a practical joke and a mild gamble. This sportsman, whom we may here call Mr. Carver, doubtless saw in these Monday auctions a golden opportunity for indulging in a caper on one or other of his hobbies. To buy some fragment of the Churchwarden's salvage, on the chance that it might prove to be real money after all, must indeed have been a gamble of irresistible charm.

One day, among the lots laid out for inspection, was a certain battered coin which, though worthless in itself, wore yet a precious jewel in its head: a vague but undeniable resemblance to a sixpence. Carver spied it, plunged wildly, and secured it for fourpence. Then, fast in the grip of his other ruling passion, he hurried to the cash desk to pay his bill. A few whispered words, and four pennorth of base metal, passed between him and that famous 'Fred' who was so much more to so many than mere manager or cashier, and Mr. Carver could then comfortably await events.

All went well. The Churchwarden, when paying in due course for his meal, placidly accepted as part of his change that same unhallowed sixpence of which he had recently so pleasurably dispossessed himself. Carver greeted him gleefully outside the door. "If that tanner is still on sale, I'll give you tuppence for it," he said. Both tanner and Churchwarden were duly sold.

TWENTY-SIX

THE MAGIC OF LLOYD'S AND THE SEEDS IT SOWED

EDWARD LLOYD, it may well be claimed, was something of a magician, a non-fictional Merlin with an astonishing gift of propagation. His greatest feat was of course to wave his wand over a Coffee-house and bid it become the World's Insurance Centre. He would no doubt have said that his 'magic' in that respect was no more than common sense and hard work. But see how Lloyd's spell persisted after his death. In the first place his surname, among the commonest half-dozen family names from Wales, was to achieve international adoption as a brand-mark indicating supreme excellence. Top steamship lines, for example, Norddeutscher Lloyd, Svenska Lloyd, Lloyd Brasileiro, and Hapag Lloyd, and at least one airline, Aero Lloyd, incorporate the name in their titles not to imply that they were in any way related to Lloyd's but that they proudly offered themselves as front-rank concerns. Visit any large city in the universe and you will find this prestigious adjective used to enrich enterprises such as 'New York Lloyd's' and 'Chicago Lloyd's' which have not the least association with the real Lloyd's of London. *Lloyd's List* [saving only the Government publication *The London Gazette*] London's oldest newspaper, born 1734, is still going strong. From *Lloyd's Register*, born 1760, sprang *Lloyd's Register of Shipping* which in turn fathered, 1834, the current establishment of that name where the building and classification of the world's ships and up-to-the-minute history of each is recorded. Here the code 'A1' at Lloyd's bestowed upon a vessel satisfying the Register's highest standards of merit gets honourable mention in the opening paragraph of the *Oxford English Dictionary* as meaning 'excellent', 'best'. It is used in that sense daily by millions, few of whom think or know of its derivation.

* * *

Born 1739, in the élite milieu of Bloomsbury and inheriting a flourishing coal business which he developed most successfully, Mr. Walter took the lead in that trade and was Chairman of the London Coal Exchange for twenty-five years. Like many wealthy merchants in the late eighteenth century he dabbled in underwriting. This side line proved so attractive that he was moved to join Lloyd's Coffee House in 1787. For twelve years fortune continued to favour him but insurance losses arising from the American War of Independence were so disastrous that after paying off his private creditors in full he went bankrupt. The remaining creditors were no doubt Lloyd's brokers who, treating him as the honourable man he was, not only left the liquidation of his estate in his own hands but presented him with his Bloomsbury mansion and its whole contents. His Lloyd's friends went even further; when Walter decided to embark on an entirely new career in the field of printing, they lent him capital enough to buy a press. He had at last found his true vocation. *Lloyd's List* was one of his earliest customers. A brace of important books in the 'best-seller' class, *Robinson Crusoe* and Burton's *Anatomy of Melancholy*, gave a boost to his reputation. Meanwhile, to keep his machines busy, he produced and published in 1788 a newspaper which he called *The Daily Universal Register*. This deservedly flourished to such an extent that competitors in several London suburbs pirated the title. To circumvent this Walter added the words 'and Times' to his paper's name and before long he changed once more to an even simpler style, *The*

Times. Thus was born, *The Thunderer*, one of the greatest and most influential newspapers ever created in any nation. And here I like to think we see again a striking manifestation of Edward Lloyd's magic wand at work.

* * *

John Julius Angerstein, born 1735, was wealthy, wise, philanthropic and deeply cultured. Lloyd's Coffee House where he took a leading part among the 'regulars' (i.e. those who paid two guineas a year for 'membership') was invaded by a class of customer whose subscribing of sheer gambling policies he saw would threaten Lloyd's good name. In 1769 he produced a drastic cure for this peril. He organised a migration of the 'regulars' from the old premises to a 'new Lloyd's' opened for them in nearby Pope's Head Alley by one of their waiters, Thomas Fielding. Two years later he led seventy-eight of his fellow members to make an even more important move. Putting up £100 each, they took a long lease of the Royal Exchange's upper floor, dropped the words 'Coffee House' from their title (although the Post Office were still using them in World War I) and so reached the durable establishment which, with two much later twentieth-century moves into even much larger premises, was destined to grow to its present immense dimensions and to face inevitably ever-increasing expansion. It was for his invaluable leadership in these vital steps which saved and consolidated the business reputation of the 'regulars' that John Julius Angerstein was and is still known as 'The Father of Lloyd's'. He died in 1823 at the ripe age of eighty-eight. The pictures he had collected with impeccable taste hung on the walls of his London mansion, 100, Pall Mall. Thirty-eight of them, including five by Claude and six of Hogarth's *Marriage à la Mode*, were bought by the Nation for £60,000 in 1824. These pictures remained on public exhibition in his Pall Mall house for a decade and then went to a neighbouring house, No. 105. Others were added by purchase and gift—a fine Titian, a Reubens, a Canaletto, a Tintoretto, a Rembrandt. In 1838 the whole collection went to its present home in the building specially erected for its reception on the site of what had been the King's Mews. Its name? The National Gallery. Is it unreasonable to see Lloyd's spell in operation once more?

* * *

In 1802 Angerstein's attention was drawn to a new practically uncapsizable and unsinkable lifeboat, the invention of one Henry Greathead. He at once realised that a fleet of them stationed at strategic points around our coasts with boats ready to render immediate aid to distressed vessels would significantly reduce the number of deaths by drowning. Accordingly he moved that Lloyd's should install such a fleet and £2,000 was then and there provided for the purpose.

During the following twenty years the lifeboats of this country, very largely supported by Lloyd's, saved innumerable imperilled lives and won world-wide praise for the gallantry and heroism with which the crews carried out this humanitarian work.

In 1824 a special body was created to take over this service. It's name? The Royal Institute for the Saving of Life from Shipwreck, later to be called The Royal National Lifeboat Institution. Another sturdy oak from Edward Lloyd's magic acorns!

* * *

When the amazing John Julius Angerstein met manifest injustice, he promptly sought a remedy. One of the most pitiable sights to be seen during the Napoleonic Wars was that of maimed and starving ex-soldiers and sailors begging for bread in the streets. Angerstein was horrified and conceived the idea that Lloyd's should find a remedy.

The remedy in this instance took the form of Lloyd's Patriotic Fund, which was launched at a meeting presided over by Lloyd's Chairman, Mr. (later Sir) Brook Watson, a former Lord Mayor of London. It may well be that the Chairman felt a special compassion for amputees because he himself had only one leg. It was resolved to raise the Fund by public subscription.

> "To animate the efforts of our Defenders by Sea and Land . . . for the purpose of assuaging the anguish of their Wounds or palliating in some degree the more weighty misfortunes of the Loss of Limbs . . . of alleviating the Distresses of the Widow and Orphan . . . of soothing the brow of Sorrow for the fall of their dearest Relatives, the props of unhappy Indigence of helpless Old Age . . . and of granting Pecuniary Rewards or Honourable Badges of Distinction for successful exertions of Valor or Merit. . . .

Lloyd's started it with a gift of £20,000, and under the influential direction of Angerstein and his friend, Sir Francis Baring, the banker, subscriptions poured in until the Fund stood at half a million sterling. Built to last and wisely administered over the years, Lloyd's Patriotic Fund has gone from strength to strength and still finds ample opportunities of helping the people contemplated by the Fund's Constitution. In World War I Lloyd's gave £45,000 while Members and Subscribers on their own made very substantial contributions to many other war charities. But even in these serious fields Lloyd's must have its bit of fun. Field-Marshal Earl Haig, seeking support for his pet scheme, 'The Officers' Association' made an appeal to the well-known generosity of Lloyd's. The then Chairman, Mr. Sidney A. Boulton, invited him to come along in person and address the Room from the caller's Rostrum. "Meanwhile," said Boulton, "I will try to collect a bit from some of the Syndicates." The Field-Marshal expressed his gratitude. Turning up two weeks later to make his speech, he received an enthusiastically noisy welcome and seemed a little shy and overcome by it. He had hardly made his opening remarks when the Chairman whispered to him, "By the way, here is your cheque." Haig took it, looked at it and as though he could not believe his eyes, examined it more closely. Then he dried up completely. The cheque was for £170,000.

* * *

Lloyd's Patriotic Fund, still in full operation, remains unique to this day, although we may look upon the Red Cross (established 1864) as a fairly close relative. No person living in our era can claim descent from Edward Lloyd. But is it too whimsical to see an aura of magic around this Coffee-man who could leave us legacies greater than those stemming from any other individual, viz.: Lloyd's of London, the world's leading Insurance Market; *The Times* (alias *The Thunderer*); *Lloyd's Register of Shipping*, enrolling the world's entire waterborne craft; England's National Picture Gallery; Lloyd's Patriotic Fund, England's greatest and oldest charity in its chosen field, and last but not least, the world's leading Lifeboat Service.

TWENTY-SEVEN

TWO LLOYD'S TYPES VERY HAPPILY REMEMBERED

OF all my good Lloyd's friends who, to my sorrow, have passed on ahead of me, I do not recall a single one who was other than a happy man. When I think of them as I so often do, they are linked in my mind with some pleasing or *outré* events in which they had taken part. I enjoy recalling two such episodes.

* * *

George Simmons was an historical figure in the sense that he was the first underwriter at Lloyd's to subscribe exclusively non-marine risks. He began using me on his claims in my early Lloyd's days, and we gradually became good friends socially. Shooting delighted him in spite of the fact that his extremely poor sight proved a mercy to the birds. He often came as a most popular guest to the shooting syndicate in which Graham Harding, Neville Manson, "Snowball" Attenborough, "Timmie" Marshall (of Bowrings) and I had guns. Among the many hundreds of cases he passed to me for attention was one in which the negligence of his assured, a rural branch railway line, was so apparent as to afford a classical example of *res ipsa loquitor* ('the thing speaks for itself'). Two trains using a single track had collided with each other violently head-on. George carried 100% of the Third Party Liability, and since there were six fatalities, it seemed obvious that he faced a disastrous total loss. Some ten days after the catastrophe when my men under command of that prince of investigators, my Mr.

W. J. Emmens, had completed their on-the-spot enquiries, George came to see me as he put it, 'for a chat'. No underwriter that I could recall had ever before called at my office about a claim, and I guessed that this railway affair must have hit him pretty hard. Spoken sympathy would not have been the done thing. But in giving a brief verbal report, I picked out a few bright spots. The Policy did not cover the railway's staff or officials; among those killed were one train driver and one railway executive. The other four fatals were among men and women with no dependents, and settlements in those instances would cost far less than might reasonably have been expected. None of the other passengers had sustained serious injuries but all had been badly shaken. One of these shock cases illustrated the vein of comedy which so often runs through a tragic situation. When the engines collided, the trains locked together, arched themselves up into the air much as a caterpillar does in travelling along. The impact tore open the floor of a lavatory compartment. A man who, at that moment, occupied the closet seat was dropped on to the track. Unharmed physically but dazed nearly to the point of unconsciousness, he crawled clear of the wreck and sat on the grass bank apparently a mere curious spectator but actually in a nightmare state, trying to gather his wits. One of the handful of peasants living in the remote and sparsely inhabited area where the accident happened running to the rescue saw this seemingly casual and uninterested onlooker and excitedly kicked him up his behind with a shouted: "For Gawd's sake, get on your feet and lend us a hand." Emmens, commiserating with this chap (who suffered more from the outrageous indignity of the kick than from his tumble) indulged his Cockney sense of humour saying, "You must count your blessings, Guv'ner—you might have been drowned."

George heard me out patiently but with apparent indifference. His only comment was: "I regard this as a total loss, William Charles, but do your best." And then, "I did not call to bother you about this railway business but about a domestic problem which faces me. The tweenie maid in our country place has fallen (and here I paraphrase) base over apex down the kitchen stairs—no broken bones—plenty of bruises and general upset—we have put her to bed—had the doctor to her. He says she will be O.K. in a week maybe. I would like you to send one of your men to advise her on her legal rights to compensation."

"But, George," said I, "in continuing to pay her full wages with board and lodging, nursing and medical attention, you are doing far more than the Workmen's Compensation Act would give her!"

"Just so," replied George, "but all the same I want your man to put her wise."

"This shall be done," said I. The railway smash faded into the insignificant background, and the tweenie maid took precedence. Her statutory right to a few shillings a week wholly overshadowed the many thousands sterling which would be sacrificed on the altar of *res ipsa loquitor*.

* * *

Easter in Paris. While our wives take their *café au lait* in bed, Graham and I take an hour's fresh air on horseback in the Bois de Boulogne. The mounts which come to the Plaza Athenée for us are none of your leather-mouthed hirelings. They are spirited Irish hunters. Graham with his smiling gift for getting the best of everything has, I suspect, left the livery stable keeper with the belief that we are leaders in the world of equitation condescendingly willing to exercise these animals for their owners, whoever they may be. We jog gently to the Etoile. A gendarme, with a grin, halts the traffic to let us pass. My mount, a little full of herself, does a Spanish Riding School *dressage* in acknowledgement. Graham also takes the salute. He is attired for the part *en vrai gentleman Anglais;* grey bowler, blue and white polka dot Ascot tie, oatmeal hacking jacket, beige breeches, gleaming top boots. We enter the Bois, an Enchanted Forest at this time of year, the sun filtering down through a ceiling of young leaves. The *piste* reserved for riders is one which Rotten Row might well envy. We trot, we canter and we slow to a walk. "You are," says Graham, "to meet in a minute or so a sweet young lady whom I met only a few days ago."

Soon we pull up in a glade where the track curves and widens a little to disclose an open shallow crescent of soft loam. In the forefront like a ballerina taking a curtain call stands a metre high solitary chestnut seedling, tender, fragile and lovely.

"*Mam'selle,*" says Graham, sweeping off his hat to her (for this is clearly his young lady), "permit me to present *mon ami m'sieur Crockière de Londres.*"

"*Enchanté, Mam'selle,*" says I, my bowler covering my heart, "*enchanté de faire votre connaissance.*"

She trembles with pleasure. This touching ceremony is never omitted from our subsequent morning rides. Nonsense? Of course! But the vernal magic of the Bois renders such playfulness fitting and acceptable or as one might say *comme il faut.*

* * *

Paris once more but later, say July 1923. We are dining and dancing and having a gay old time at *Le Caveau Caucassien,* the plushiest of all the new White Russian restaurants. Arthur J. ("Jack") Campbell (head of Toplis and Harding, Paris and its many European branches) with his sweet Genevoise wife, Valentine, are host and hostess. Graham and his wife and I with mine make up the rest of the party. We are all in a festive mood. The food and service are superb, the music just right and the usual minute dance floor is intimately *en suite*. Is the handsome Cossack who sings so delightfully to the guests an exiled Russian noble, even a Romanoff? This could be; some no less exalted are driving taxis and glad of the chance. This is one of the jolliest parties ever. We beam when Graham rises to offer a final toast. "We are," says he, "the proud parents of beautiful children, all girls. Is it not time for us to have sons and heirs? I beseech you, darling ladies, to give this matter serious thought and meanwhile, here's to your continued good health and happiness.

* * *

Two years pass by. Nature having accepted Graham's challenge rewards him, Jack and me with bonny sons and heirs all born within a few months of one another.

* * *

Graham is in U.S.A. during Prohibition. Some of his New York staff call at his hotel, bringing with them a gift rare indeed at that time, nothing less than a bottle of non-vintage Bollinger. When Graham opens it for them in the secrecy of his bedroom, he has but loosened the cork when with a deafening bang, it shoots out like a shell from a field gun. He is horrified to see that the 'champagne' spilled over the dressing-table has removed the varnish. Agreed *nem. con.* that the drink shall be something else and less lethal.

* * *

The scene changes to Illinois. The Chicago staff, a trio, offer Graham a repetition of his New York welcome with, to his horror, that same non-vintage Bollinger. Graham, long on tact, says, "You really should not go to all this expense on my behalf—but allow me!" He eases out the cork over the bath-tub, making sure that at least half the 'champagne' goes down the waste. Full of apologies for this clumsiness, he pours glasses for the three visitors and a shallow one for himself. He sips the wine and once again is horrified. This is indeed the veritable Bollinger.

* * *

Another twist of the kaleidoscope. We see a young man at the front door of a Maida Vale mansion. It is 2 a.m. He wears a pierrot costume in black with white pompoms, a pleated ruff and a clown's hat. He is writhing in corkscrew fashion as though in pain. A patrolling P.C. comes up quietly and shines his lamp upon this odd spectacle.

"Wot's agoin' on 'ere?" he asks.

The young man stammers, "I hired this damn pierrot outfit to wear over my dress clothes for the Covent Garden Ball. My latch-key is in my left trouser pocket and this costume has no pockets, only a short slit down the right leg. I have been struggling to get my hand through that damn slit round to my left trouser pocket, and I can't quite make it."

"Who are you, Guv?" asks the copper.

"Harding," says Graham, "and I live here."

"Better ring the bell and get someone down," says the copper.

"I should hate to do that," says Graham. "It would awaken my wife. She would be furious!"

The P.C. with a philosophic shrug pushes the bell button. A few minutes go by. The door is opened by Mrs. Harding evidencing considerable displeasure. She admits reluctantly that Graham is her husband and lets him in. Removing his ridiculous hat, Graham enters and does his best to assuage the marital wrath. But the lady sweeps upstairs, cursing under her breath in a not too ladylike fashion. Poor Graham stands still to think things over. Suddenly the silence of his meditations is broken by a metallic tinkle. Something has dropped on to the hall's marble paving. It is the latch-key!

EPILOGUE

THE massive silver plate with which Lloyd's honoured Admiral Lord Nelson and his fellow officers was given to salute their triumphant Battles at Sea. The silver trophies with which Lloyd's honoured me, the scale model fire engine and the antique tea service, saluted two of my Battles on Land—the Fire Case of 1933 and an Australian Mission of 1954. These gifts, most highly prized, are in a class by themselves. Beside them must be put the fifty-year-long stream of 'curly' claims with which underwriters fed my insatiable appetite for gentlemanly detection.

Nothing could be more comforting for a lawyer out at grass in retirement than fond memories of past cases. The story of one such case I now offer in a spirit of gratitude and by way of epilogue to the foregoing rambling chapters mostly in lighter vein about Lloyd's men and their doings.

OLD MOTHER HUBBARD

I once had the joy of giving lunch to that delightful writer W. W. Jacobs. At his own choice the talk, which went on for hours after the meal had ended, was about crime. He pumped me non-stop for yarns of insurance frauds. To my great content this meeting led to an exchange of letters. He promised that in the spring he would see Lloyd's in my company. "For the time being (he wrote) I take my breakfast in bed and listen to the one o'clock news. How is arson going?" I replied that astute merchants did not go in for fire raising when trade was brisk and stock was worth more than had been paid for it; faked jewellery losses were a more lucrative 'lay'. "If you fire your warehouse (I said) and for some reason or other the Insurers escape liability you are out of pocket to the extent of the damage done. Whereas if the Insurers refuse to pay on a dud jewellery claim you still have your jewellery!" His answer to that was: "Thank you so much for your well-meant hint but alas! I have no jewellery."

This was during World War II when it was not the done thing for ladies to go about heavily adorned with gems. Thus there was nothing to cause suspicion when a certain 'Mrs. 'B.' asked her Lloyd's brokers to insure a £5,000 single-stone diamond ring for her and to say nothing about it to her husband who did not approve of her wearing jewellery in wartime. Underwriters do not find personal jewellery insurance profitable. There is little enough to be made even from Policies granted to staid proposers of stainless respectability. Careless ladies with a bad history of losses are almost uninsurable. Apparently, however, Mrs. B.' was not careless; she had sustained, she said, "only one very small loss during the last few years". She got her cover and in so doing raised the curtain on a comedy which W.W.J. would have relished to the full had he lived to see it out.

When Mrs. 'B.'s' policy was but a day old, the diamond ring was lost. She had absentmindedly left it behind with an eternity ring—in the lavatory of a London hotel after washing her hands. Someone must then have stolen it. My old friends Toplis and Harding were called in to act for the underwriters. They and I, over the years, have hunted in couples on many an amusing job. I like to tell this story for several reasons, but mainly because it supports one of my deepest beliefs, that lucks rewards persistence.

Mrs. 'B.' when reporting her loss to the Police said that she bought the ring in London in 1939 from a Paris jeweller named Bensimon. Later when pressed for evidence of the purchase, a paid cheque, a receipt or something specific of the kind, Mrs. 'B' changed her tale; she had not *bought* the ring from Bensimon she had given him other articles of jewellery in exchange and therefore no such written evidence as we sought was to be expected. We could see no chance of checking this, Paris being at that time in German occupation.

But coincidence came to our aid. Working on the London staff of Toplis and Harding was a Mr. Gregory who had been evacuated from their Paris office under the threat of the enemy advance. He recalled that in 1938 Mrs. 'B.' (who at that time was quite properly a Mrs. Somebody else) had claimed on Lloyd's for a diamond brooch stolen from her handbag in Monte Carlo. It had fallen to him in the Paris Office to handle that loss for underwriters. His file relating to it was, of course, still in Paris. But he remembered having written London Office describing the brooch so that routine enquiries might be made of the Maidenhead firm from whom it was said to have been bought. His letter preserved on the London file showed that the main stone in the Monte Carlo brooch had been 'one large pear-shaped Brilliant—16·4 carats'. That description might have applied equally well to the pear-shaped brilliant 'approximately 17 carats' in the ring now the subject of the alleged hotel loss. Was it possible that the Monte Carlo diamond and the hotel diamond were one and the same?

Wandering through Soho Gregory encountered a fellow evacuee. Over a cup of coffee they discussed the adventures and whereabouts of mutual acquaintances; the friend spoke of his neighbour, a Hebrew, who, escaping liquidation at the hands of the Nazis, had reached America. He was a jeweller of high repute and a member of the British Antique Dealers' Association. His name was Gaston Bensimon.

Enquiry at the Antique Dealers' Association told me that

Bensimon was living at St. Regis Hotel, New York. Interviewed there by our agent he said he had never at any time dealt with Mrs. 'B' and, was not in London when that lady said she had there acquired the ring from him. Meanwhile a discreet circular to other assessors had given us proof that Mrs. 'B.'s' declaration of "only one very small loss during the last few years" was, to put it politely, an understatement. She had collected from her insurers between 1937 and 1939 nearly £7,000 on five losses of which the Monte Carlo loss alone stood at £3,965.

The assured who advances a dishonest claim commonly pretends great indignation if that claim is not met at once. Mrs. 'B.' ran true to type. Putting on a show of anger at the impertinence of our probing she rushed off to a solicitor. One may assume he advised that her reticence about the earlier losses when seeking the insurance, could make the Policy in law so much waste paper. He wisely threw himself upon the mercy of underwriters whose tolerance he knew to be almost illimitable.

We were, although he did not know it, holding all the trumps, the ace being the unexpectedly alive and upright jeweller in New York. It cost us nothing to tell the solicitor that if he could prove to his own satisfaction how, when and where Mrs. 'B.' had acquired both the 'Monte Carlo' and the 'Hotel' diamonds, he might be sure Lloyd's would stretch a benevolent eye towards the carelessness with which she had handled the truth regarding her earlier Insurance history.

It must have dismayed the lady to find that her own solicitor, from whom she hoped so much, was now insisting no less strongly than we upon proofs which she could not give. Here was a dilemma. On the one hand all chances of picking up from the underwriters what had once looked like an easy £5,000, if her previous experience with them was anything to go by, had vanished. On the other she could not just admit defeat, 'find' the ring and as though nothing had happened resume wearing it.

* * *

Some two months later the hotel received through the post, but unstamped, a brown paper parcel just small enough to enter a pillar-box. The address on it had been made up by gumming on to the cover printed letters cut from various publications. Inside the package was a shallow cardboard box which held seven sheets of rough paper on to which had been laboriously gummed, words and letters in many styles to convey the following message:

> "Please Deliver the parcel at once stolen property Dear Sir we have just lost our Doughter who died From consumtion She told us The Terrible TRUTH About The Stolen property at your Hotel How She was waulking in To the Lavatory near the drinking place saw the Two RINGS ends a Wach Put them in Her bag went away in hurry This was LAST winter Old Mother and i knew nothing the Poor dear was always crasy about Fancie ORNEMENS We head some Truble Before the old woman went to the Police to tell them all about "Bless my soul" She got terrified said, afraid of will arrest her. That would be very hard to We are very poor people efford running risk loosing Our job Well, sir, may we have your forgiveness all the Truble."

The box also contained Mrs. 'B.'s' diamond ring, her eternity ring and a self-winding oblong pocket watch. The anonymous sender of the package was obviously Mrs. 'B.' herself. The introduction of the pocket watch the loss of which had never before been mentioned, was to let us see with what an artless creature we were dealing. She had clean forgotten putting her watch on the basin with the other things! It was no doubt her belief that upon receipt of the parcel the hoteliers would at once give her the news and invite her to call and collect. The claim on Lloyd's would be withdrawn without embarrassment and the pear-shaped diamond could go back into circulation.

But we had other views about that pear-shaped diamond. After its 'loss' at Monte Carlo Mrs. 'B.'s' story was that she had bought it from certain jewellers in Maidenhead. This was a lie. The truth, as we discovered, was that she had only taken it to them to be made up into a brooch. Their craftsman who did the mounting had long since left but we ran him to earth in a munitions factory. On his Sunday off he met me at the hotel and examined Mrs. 'B.'s' ring. Without hesitation he identified its pear-shaped diamond as the stone which had gone into the brooch.

It was decided that for the moment nothing should be said to Mrs. 'B.' about the return of the jewellery. Having wholly avoided the hotel since her 'loss' she now began to haunt it and to greet its executives expecting that one of them would sooner or later exclaim, "Wonderful news, Madam, your rings are back!" She showed alarm when no such news was forthcoming. She may well have thought that one very cunning move in her scheme had gone wrong. There are two classes of mail over which Post Offices watch with especial care; registered packages and packages which are mailed insufficiently stamped. The cynic may be excused for thinking that an unstamped or insufficiently stamped package on which there is 'fourpence to pay' receives from the postman, who is under a duty to collect that fourpence, greater attention than he gives registered mail for which the customer had paid cash in advance. Mrs. 'B.', a business woman with little to learn in matters of this kind, had carried the anonymity of her package to the point of posting it with no stamps whatever, relying, as she felt she could, upon the zeal of our postal services to deliver it safely not for her sake but for the sake of the postage due. Why then did the hotel tell her nothing? Was it possible that in this instance the Post Office had applied some new rule, perhaps because jewellery was involved, and that her parcel was held in Mount Pleasant?

She had good reason to feel uneasy. We left her to suffer while we tried our best to pin her down as the sender of that parcel. It was unlikely that whoever gummed the message together could have done so without leaving finger-prints on it. We found none. Expert examination disclosed that the gummer had worn rubber gloves, perhaps for no better reason than to avoid getting gummy hands.

One did not need to be a Sherlock Holmes to deduce that the words and letters used in the message had mostly come from a book of nursery rhymes in which 'Old Mother Hubbard' played her part. It was not impossible that the remnants of the book were still lying around in Mrs. 'B.'s' house. One of my helpers by unorthodox but legitimate means searched that house from cellar to garret. The nearest he got to a mutilated book of rhymes was a small heap of ash from paper which had been recently burned beyond recognition under the greenhouse boiler. But we traced a domestic, a cook who had recently walked out from Mrs. 'B.'s' service in a state of justifiable indignation. It had been alleged that a story book or picture book which had been left by Mrs. 'B.' in the kitchen had disappeared. There was 'quite a row' about it. The book it was said had been bought as a birthday present for a niece and something else had to be bought in substitution. Moreover, contemporaneously with the alleged disappearance of the book a sixpenny pot of Woolworth's gum had been taken from its home in the kitchen for the purpose of 'sticking on labels' and had not come back. Here was the over-elaboration which one finds so often in amateur fraud. Says Mrs. 'B.' to herself (after using up

'Old Mother Hubbard' for the hotel message): "It may be found that I recently bought that very book! I must make a fuss about its disappearance." And so she prepared what Hollywood calls an 'alibi' and was nearly betrayed by it. The worthy cook, had she shown a little more curiosity, might have learned enough to put her unreasonably irascible mistress in jeopardy.

But Mrs. 'B.'s' luck had not deserted her. I never knew where the book was bought; nor to this day, among all the thousands of forms in which this 150-year-old nursery rhyme has appeared, have I run across the edition which Mrs. 'B.' used for her gummy purpose. Nor could I prove to demonstration the part which Mrs. 'B.' had played in the return of the jewellery in its unstamped package. This, while disappointing, was unimportant because I held the thirteenth trump; the diamond. I sent it to Scotland Yard with a formal claim that it belonged to the underwriters who had paid for its alleged loss in Monte Carlo. Mrs. 'B.', notified of this, said it was ridiculous to pretend that this was the Monte Carlo stone; it was the hotel stone entirely different and it belonged to her. In view of this disputed ownership she was invited to go to the Courts for a decision. Or as an alternative would the lady care to pay the Monte Carlo underwriters £1,000 to stand aside? Underwriters had paid her for that stone after the Monte Carlo adventure £3,965. By the time it figured in the hotel loss its value, at any rate for insurance purposes, had jumped to £5,000. Why should we offer to sell it back to her for a fifth of that sum? The answer is that before sending the stone to Scotland Yard I had it unmounted and valued by experts. They found it light in weight and so poor in quality that £1,000 was about all I should have been bid in the trade. In the circumstances I felt a deal at that figure was fitting and I let Mrs. 'B.', an unwilling buyer at that price, repossess the diamond which had meant so much to her.

While the last act of this comedy was playing itself out the life of W. W. Jacobs, then in his eightieth year, was drawing to its close. He died before I had a chance to tell him that my early letter had gone too far when it implied that if insurers refuse to pay on a fraudulent jewellery claim the assured *always* retains the jewellery and is therefore not out of pocket.